Claire,

all cute, witty women
I know that wear glasses
are secretly dirty and
want their face licked
Real Bad!

XOXO,
Eve Maye

Get It Girl Guide

to
Online Dating
& Sextiquette™

Get It Girl Guide

to
Online Dating
& Sextiquette™

Eve Mayer

BROWN BOOKS
PUBLISHING GROUP

Get It Girl Guide to Online Dating and Sextiquette™

Brown Books Publishing Group
16250 Knoll Trail Drive, Suite 205
Dallas, Texas 75248
www.BrownBooks.com
(972) 381-0009

A New Era in Publishing™

ISBN 978-1-61254-162-4
LCCN 2013957651

Printed in the United States
10 9 8 7 6 5 4 3 2 1

For more information or to contact the author, please go to www.GetItGirlGuide.com or www.Sextiquette.com

This book is dedicated

To every single woman who
chooses to run toward fear.

To my future boyfriend(s), buckle
up; it's gonna be a wild ride!

Contents

Acknowledgments

Thank you to the center of my life, my daughter, Mia Mayer Orsburn. I love you.

Thank you to my parents. For my Dad, who encouraged me to write this book. For my Mom, who supports me through every crazy idea I have.

Thank you to my girlfriends present, past, and future Maria Martinez, Ruth Ferguson, Toni Williams, Mary B. Adams, Melisse Meza, Angela Schmidt, Paige Schmidt, Claire Kojis, Brisa Castillo, Elizabeth Murdock, Lisa Wigger, Silvia Irani, Katia Reeb, Jenni Linzey Scheffler, Shannon Streater, Dianna Slaton, Carrie Houston, and Angie Smith.

Thank you to all my friends who supported me in creating this book, including Craig Isaac, Tom Niesen, Glenn Baldwin, Michelle Robertson, Monica Coney, Mark Winters, David Hammer, Ken Lowe, Michael Holmes, Pam Gerber, Bob McPherrin, David Bell, Michael Collins, Sashe Dimitroff, Betsy Atwood, Wes Atwood, and especially Jason Brake.

Thanks to these lovely ladies and their pussy cat pictures: Melanie Morgan, Sally Cloonan, Dawn Shiley.

Thank you to Milli Brown, the Brown Book Publishing crew, and Social Media Delivered staff in making this dream a reality. Thanks to Jamie Nanquil for the illustrations in this book.

Thank you to all twenty-eight dudes I dated—with special thanks to the super lame ones and the super hot ones.

Why Listen to Me?

You're probably asking yourself, "What does she know?"

Heck, I don't blame you. I'd be skeptical too. Let me just make this clear from the get-go: I'm not a therapist, counselor, doctor, or sexologist. I'm not even a yoga instructor. And I don't do a trapeze act like Pink, although I wish I could.

Chances are I'm a lot like your best girlfriend (or the one you wish you had), who listens, makes you laugh, offers good advice and does it in a way that cracks you up. You know the one who says what everybody else is thinking— that's me.

I'm thirty-nine years old. Maybe you're ten years younger or twenty years older. It doesn't matter. The same rules apply.

I'm a mom with one child, married once, and divorced after a fourteen-year relationship. I never imagined I'd be dating again. Maybe you've never been married or you're twice divorced. You might have no kids or eight of them. What I've learned still applies.

I have wrinkles, and I wish my boobs were riding as high as they used to. My hair is probably wilder and frizzier than yours. Chances are you cook way better and run faster than I do. That's a cinch, because I barely cook and don't run at all. Your feet are probably smaller than mine, and I'm likely bigger than you. I mean, there is a number two in my dress size, but it isn't the *only* number.

I own a social media company, and I do a lot of traveling and public speaking, so I bet we're both hardworking women (either at home, at the office, or both). And we're both really, really busy. All this to say, we may not share the same stats, but we're a lot alike.

As a business owner, I've learned that goal setting is critical to success. Dating is a numbers game, so I set a goal for myself. My original goal was to go on fifty-two dates in one year. They could be first dates, second dates, or more. I didn't care about that. I just wanted to average one date per week. That sounded doable. If I really liked someone, I could date them repeatedly and still work toward my goal.

My friends think my goal setting is a bit nuts, but setting and achieving goals keep me happy and focused. Plus I'm good at it. Hell, I'm an overachiever. In fact, I'm such an overachiever I hit my dating goal in nine months! This kind of makes sense if you think about it. If women can create an entire human being in nine months, surely we can go on fifty-two dates in the same amount of time. Really. How hard can dating be?

Here are my numbers: From January third (the day after my divorce was final) through September 30, I went on fifty-nine dates with twenty-eight different men. The vast majority of men lasted one date, and sometimes the date was so bad they barely lasted through that. There were ten guys I dated more than once. The most dates I went on with any one dude were ten. Yes, that's a lot of men, and yes, I enjoyed myself thoroughly.

Fifty-nine dates may sound like too much for you, or you might think I'm a lightweight. We're not all going to have the same goals, and that doesn't matter either. To achieve my goal, I had to overcome my ignorance and terror of online dating, dating in general, flirting, sexting, and everything else that goes along with being single in this day and age. Despite my crushing fear of being newly single, I conquered the world of online dating and hit my numbers.

I met some losers, lots of average Joes, and a few winners. I didn't come out of this one-year process with a husband. I wasn't looking for one. Not yet. I just wanted to go on fun dates, stay safe, and enjoy.

Whether you're a longtime single or new at this game, if you want to enjoy dating, this book is for you. If your goal is to have a man for life, a man for a few weeks, or a man for tonight, this book is for you. If the thought of dating makes you cringe and you can't remember the last time you went on a date, felt confident on a date, or laughed about one, this book is certainly for you.

Once Upon a Time Warp

He was tall and handsome, and his plaid, buttoned-down shirt was a little too tight—just the way I like it. I had not dated for fourteen years, and at the first sight of him, I couldn't breathe or speak. We went into the coffeehouse and sat down at a table in the corner. Having heard the horror stories about online dating, I was ready for disaster to unfold. I was sure he'd be secretly married, was going to drug me to steal my organs then sell them on the black market, or worse—just not be into me. At the very least, he'd have a really bad case of halitosis.

I was wrong. He was hot. Hell, he even had hair—the good kind that grows on top of a man's head, not the bad kind that grows on a man's back or butt. He was intelligent in a weird kind of way that I found intriguing. And oh, man, he was funny in a sick kind of way that is right up my alley.

We talked for a couple of hours that day and dated for several weeks.

When he learned he was the first person I'd met online, he warned me. "You have no idea what online dating is really like. You're like an undefeated fighter who's only experienced victory."

I didn't believe him. This online dating thing was going to be easy. As it turned out, he was right, and I was wrong. So very wrong. Online dating is a bitch. Once I figured that out, I swore I'd make it *my* bitch!

Clearly the singles market has gone crazy over the past fourteen years. What the hell was happening out there while I was busy being married and raising a kid? It's like that Brendan Frazer movie, *Blast from the Past*, where he climbs out of a fallout shelter after thirty-five years to find the world is oh-so-different.

I'm pretty sure spanking and hair pulling in the bedroom were the exception, not the expectation, fourteen years ago. Today they're so common TI's rapping about them and much worse on Robin Thicke's "Blurred Lines." And if you haven't read *Fifty Shades of Grey*, you have no idea what naughty things people are fantasizing about doing in the bedroom. I haven't had time to read it (too busy dating!), but I googled it and read the dirty parts online.

Back then, none of my friends was getting her junk vajazzled (bedazzling her lady parts with glitter or fake jewels). Just imagine having rhinestones glued to your business. OK, maybe it'll make your kitty look pretty, but if someone grinds on you real good, they may end up with injuries. And what if one of those gems comes off? If you can't find it, you'll be thinking, uh-oh, my vagina is a gem mine waiting to be discovered. Do you really want Snow White's dwarves in there singing, "Hi ho, hi ho, it's off to work we go?" I don't think so.

Soon after I became single again, Maria and two other girlfriends took me for my first bikini wax. This was news to me, but they told me guys now want—no, *expect*—a woman's junk to be as bare as a baby's butt. Either that or the hair around the nether regions gets waxed into creative shapes like a martini glass, a heart, or a smiley face. Being the nonconformist I am, I wanted something different. I considered requesting a trapezoid, but then I thought better of it.

I don't like to do things half assed (and by the way, the ass is often included in the waxing), so I opted for the full treatment. The Kojak, as it was called, was guaranteed to leave everything bare and smooth. "Don't do it! You're a novice. You won't be able to handle it!" Maria warned me. But I knew I was a badass. Bring it on!

I took some ibuprofen and drank some champagne, as directed, and I entered a small room that looked like a doctor's office, complete with examining table. After I stripped from the waist down, a woman with a devious smile and strong accent strode in. She ordered me to put my body in various positions so awkward I've never even attempted them during sex. At first, I couldn't tell where she was from, but after she covered my vagina with hot wax and ripped those strips, I knew she was from hell.

I don't remember people talking about anal bleaching fourteen years ago. Seriously why does this even need to happen? Don't people know not to judge others by the color of their skin? Is the anus subject to a different set of rules that I'm unaware of? What makes a bleached anus more desirable than a dark anus anyway? And what's the optimal shade on the anal attractiveness meter? Do I need to take in a paint swatch from Sherwin-Williams?

I started dating my ex-husband when I was twenty-five and he was thirty-one. Among the couples I knew then, most of the men were older than or about the same age as their wives. Apparently, while I was married, a revolution swept the nation and cougars were born. Thank you, Ashton and Demi.

Recently Tina Turner, who is seventy-three years old, married a fifty-seven-year-old, and forty-four-year-old Jennifer Lopez has a boyfriend who is twenty-five. I am now thirty-nine, and I was shocked the first time a twenty-nine-year-old asked to meet me. He told me how hot older women are. I had no idea, but I'm darn thankful I got old right when it became cool. Do I date younger men? Heck yes. Is it hot? Darn right it is. As a firm believer in equal rights, why shouldn't I walk around with younger eye candy on my arm? I should! And if it floats your boat, so should you. Plus it really makes sense if you think about it. Women tend to live longer than men, so if you choose a younger man to grow old with, there's a better chance you'll die around the same time.

Like any good thing, however, there is a limit. A nineteen-year-old once asked me out, and I had to say no because, well, eww. For me, if there's a possibility I could have breastfed my date when he was a baby, I have to pass. How you determine when it's eww and when it's hot is entirely up to you.

Chapter 2

Girl, Know Thyself

So you're one brave girl, and you're ready to foray into the adventurous world of online *amore*. First things first: Begin with the happy ending in mind.

What do you want out of this?

"I want a man!" you say. Hang on for a minute. Think about what you really want—knowing that will help you navigate this process. More than likely, you fit into one of the five different personality types who use online dating sites. I'll elaborate in a sec, but first it's important to remember that you're not locked into any one of these. Over time, you may switch personalities, depending on your wants and needs. For example, I'm currently a Dater, but one day I'll probably be a Knotter.

The Friendster

The Friendster's goal for online dating is not dating. The Friendster wants to increase his or her social activity and make new friends (male or female). Friendsters are not looking for friends with benefits (FWBs)—those you have sex with.

Expanding your social circle is a great goal but not via online dating sites. Some online dating profiles will specify "looking for new friends," but the majority of people using dating sites are interested in something other than friendship. If you're a Friendster, online dating sites aren't for you.

The Chatter

The Chatter's goal is simply to find people to converse with online. They don't want to meet or date. Chatters keep the relationship 100 percent online and never meet face to face. I was really surprised to find a lot of men who were Chatters. I couldn't understand why they would talk, flirt, try to build real rapport, and then refuse to meet in person.

A friend suggested they might be married. Could be. There are, however, some Chatters who simply prefer a virtual relationship. They may not feel confident or safe enough to engage with someone in person. If your goal is to build an online relationship that will never transition to face-to-face, you're a Chatter. There are men out there who are looking for the same thing, but you'll run into a lot of guys who will get frustrated with you and insist that you meet in person eventually. To avoid any misunderstandings, you'd better make clear in your profile that you're just online to chat and you intend to keep it that way.

The Banger

The Banger's goal for online dating is sex. Bangers aren't looking for a date or a relationship. They simply want someone to warm the bed or the back seat of the car or the Burger King restroom. Certain online dating sites cater to Bangers, but they can find plenty of action on mainstream dating sites as well. Bangers come in two varieties:

One-time Bangers are looking for a new person every time.

Repeat Bangers, aka FWBs, want someone they can get down and dirty with over and over again on separate occasions.

You might assume that all Bangers are men, but that's not true. Some women get tired of being in relationships or simply aren't interested in investing in one. If you're a Banger, that's OK. It just means your dating goal right now is finding Mr. Tonight, not Mr. Forever.

The Dater

The Dater's goal is just what it sounds like—to date. The majority of people on most of the mainstream dating sites are Daters. There are two types:

The Serial Dater is looking for people to go out on one or two or three dates with but has no intention of getting into a relationship (not to be confused with the cereal dater, who wants dates that end with Cheerios for breakfast). The Serial Dater sees dating as an ongoing activity, not a means to an end.

The Relationship Dater is going on dates to find a relationship and likely has a list of qualities in mind that the ideal mate would possess.

The Dater may or may not engage in sexual activity. Banging, therefore, is just a side note (although a very enjoyable side note) for the Dater.

The Knotter

The Knotter's goal for online dating is to find a soul mate and enter into a long-term relationship to tie the knot. A Knotter feels a committed relationship is important, even essential. Knotters are motivated to get to know people as quickly as possible. They usually have a very detailed list of qualifications a potential partner must meet. The Knotter is much like The Relationship Dater, but the timeline is compressed. The pressure is on to reach the end goal. Knotters can sometimes scare potential mates away with their urgency. When two Knotters meet and hit it off, though, things usually move at the speed of light.

Woman, know thyself. Figure out which one of these five you are. You will save hours of grief sitting across from a Knotter who's already planting the rose garden and painting the picket fence, while you're dreaming of getting properly laid and going home alone for a good night's sleep.

Chapter 3

Put Yourself First, and Go for It

When I was growing up, I assumed that my mom had put her life on hold because of her love for me. There were times we didn't have much money, but I never wanted for anything. I had the best furniture, clothes, and lessons and attended the best private school in the area (which wasn't cheap). I was an only child, and my mom—and dad too—believed I came first. My parents were young, intelligent, ambitious, and in love. Both of them had a killer sense of humor. I had an amazing childhood, and thanks to that upbringing, I truly enjoy being the person I am today.

Nevertheless, I often wondered why I had new outfits every season while my mom wore the same clothes year after year. I wondered why I had fancy Ethan Allen furniture in my bedroom while my parents had the same old bed and mattress forever. They believed in doing everything they could for me at their own sacrifice.

Now that I have a daughter, she's the center of my life, but to be the best mom and role model I can be, I believe I have to put myself first. I must be a fulfilled and empowered woman so she can grow up to be one as well. I want her to feel that she's the center of my life, but I don't want her to believe that I don't value my own life and experiences. That's why, even though I love vacations with my daughter, I also take one on my own each year. And I'll admit it's way more fun to buy clothes for my daughter, but every few months, I indulge in a new piece of clothing for myself too.

I run into many women who are devoted mothers, loving daughters, and hardworking professionals. They're so busy putting others first, they feel they must wait until later to date. I ask you: When is later?

"I'll date when the kids are older . . . when Mom gets better . . . when I make partner at my job . . . when I lose twenty pounds . . . . That's when I'll finally date and find that partner I want to have in my life."

I watch these women wait and wait and wait until the kids leave for college, their moms pass away, they finally do make partner (or get passed over for someone else), they lose some weight (or not). Then do they start dating? Heck no! Now they say they're too old, too out-of-practice, or the dating scene has changed too much. They never even go after what they want, and they end up alone.

There's nothing wrong with being alone. In fact, I rather enjoy it. Many people prefer it as a permanent lifestyle choice. I'm speaking to the women who don't want to be alone forever, the women who want a lover, a boyfriend, or a husband. Here's what I have to say: Stop putting everyone else first. Put yourself first, and go for it!

When my divorce was finalized, I waited exactly one day before going out on a date. Was I scared? You're damn right I was scared, and that was exactly why I didn't wait. The excuses I could have made were too tempting—my adorable daughter, my growing company, my sick mom—and I knew that if I started making excuses, I would never stop.

Instead I chose to run toward my fear. And I want you to do the same.

15

Think about it. You will never ever be younger than you are right now. Unless you have a boatload of money for some serious Botox or plastic surgery, you're never going to have fewer wrinkles than you do now. And if you take a realistic look at your history in terms of weight, chances are you may never lose those twenty extra pounds you've carried around for the past twenty years.

Your excuses are fictions, and only you have the power to stop making them up. I chose not to fall back on those stories and deal in realities. As a result, I date often and enjoy the kind of attention from men I want while running a successful company, helping out with my mom, and raising one of the most amazing six-year-olds in the world. You can do it too. It just takes guts.

Chapter 4

The "Wonderful" Truth about Divorce

At 10:30 this morning, I was still in bed. There may have been someone quite young, handsome, and sweet who kept me up for most of the night in a very good way. I'm just not saying.

Now I'm at my favorite coffeehouse writing this chapter before I head out to my one-and-a-half-hour massage and eyelash extension appointment, followed by dinner with extended family and later drinks with friends. Did a Saturday like this ever happen when I was married? Hell no!

Here's the truth about divorce: It's exactly what you make of it.

When I was married, I wanted to redecorate my house, but my husband and I couldn't agree on anything. Now I decorate my house any way I want to.

When I was married, I felt obligated to be home with my husband on nights I should have been out to dinner with friends, giggling with the girls, and nurturing those important relationships.

When I was married, my daughter woke me up at 6:00 every morning. Now, because I share custody with my ex, who is an excellent dad, I get to sleep until eight or even ten once or twice a week.

When I was married, we parented together, and we had to compromise on the rules. Today we continue to do a great job at co-parenting, but my daughter follows her dad's rules at his house and my rules at mine, and I like that.

When I was married, we rarely entertained. Now I have parties at my house and go out more. Best of all, the television remote is mine all mine!

Do I think I'll be married again one day? Yes, I do. There's so much about marriage I respect, value, and enjoy. But I'm not in a hurry. There are too many delicious things about this single life to savor. While I'm single, I'll continue to milk every little bit of pleasure out of it. And when I get married again, I'll do a better job of holding on to some of the pleasures I've grown accustomed to in my single life.

I'm not pushing divorce. I'm simply giving a reality check to those of you who've been through the breakup of a long-term relationship. Your new life can be great but only if you choose to make it that way. I do understand that the circumstances that led to my divorce were not typical. There was no cheating and no terrible treatment of each other. We had a very good marriage for about seven years, but the next seven years took us in different directions, and over time, we fell out of love. Even so, going through a divorce was horrendously painful. I cried for months, and I'm not a crier. I felt like a failure, and I suck at failing. I wondered if I would ever be able to date again, have sex again, flirt again, or love again. I thought that maybe my life was over. In reality, life was just beginning again.

When bad things happen, we have a choice. We can get caught up in the pain and live in the shadow of the past, or we can step into the light of a brand new life full of possibilities.

I choose the light.

My family was surprised when I started dating right away. "Don't you want to take time to get to know yourself?" Um, what? Get to know myself? Oh, I know myself very well, and every day I get to know myself a little better.

My therapist wasn't surprised when I was ready to date right away. She knew I had a strong sense of who I was and what I wanted. She knew that I had been reading, meditating, and working for years on becoming the person I wanted to be. By the way, hell yes, I go to therapy, and I think you should too, not because I think you're nuts, but because we can all learn how to live better, make ourselves happier, and lead kinder lives. Eventually your friends are going to get sick of you whining all the time and not paying them for listening to your annoying crap, especially if you aren't doing anything about it.

At first, my friends pitied me after my divorce. I couldn't have gotten through it without them. But once I got over the pain, excitement began to build up inside of me, and I began to imagine what it would be like to flirt with a man again, have dinner with a man again, caress a man's hair again, hug a man just a little too long again, and kiss a man again. After all, I'd been tied to the same one for fourteen years. To be honest, freedom sounded terrifyingly delicious.

One of the reasons I started dating right away was fear. I was scared of being like so many other women I've known who divorced and never dated again. I watched their ex-husbands date and often remarry while the women stayed lonely and miserable and talked about the day when circumstances would be ideal and they'd date again. All too often that day never came. I was terrified of ending up like that, and I decided to run toward the fear.

For many divorced women, that fear of dating again is paralyzing. Though they have a desire to date again, they're afraid to take action. So they do nothing and expect Prince Charming or the milkman to show up. There are two things I know for sure:

There is no Prince Charming.

The milkman doesn't come to your house any more. Your chances of getting a date without taking control of the situation are slim to none.

If you've been through divorce or a bad breakup, I'm truly sorry. But it's time to allow yourself to let that pain go and squeeze every ounce of joy out of the life you have, while building the life you want.

Pain is temporary. Joy is temporary. You choose whether to wallow in pain or embrace joy.

Psst! Choose joy! ;)

Chapter 5

The Beyonce Factor:
Building Your Fearless Alter Ego

You've heard of the Drag Queen Name Game. You know—combine the name of your first pet with the name of the street you grew up on and *voilà*! It's fun but pretty much useless until you decide finally to start up your drag queen act. There's another name game that I find not only useful but absolutely necessary for survival in the dating game and in life in general. It's called Fearless Alter Ego (FAE).

I created my FAE name after reading an article about Beyonce. (And who the heck doesn't love and admire Beyonce?) She's gorgeous, talented, and intelligent as well as a good daughter, a wife, a mom, and a superstar. She also has one of the most rockin' bods I've ever seen. To say I admire her is an understatement. I see her perform and marvel at her self-confidence. Yet, according to an article I read, Beyonce is very shy.

After all her success, Beyonce still gets extremely nervous before going in front of a crowd. To get over her fear, she created a brave and sassy alter ego named Sasha Fierce, and it's Sasha, not Beyonce, who's a sexy superstar shaking her hips and belting out hits. Obviously it works for her.

This is the Beyonce Factor.

I wanted to start dating as soon as my divorce was final, but I was terrified. How was I going to have the courage to create an online dating profile and then actually go on a date? I wouldn't know the first thing to say to a new guy. I'd forgotten how to flirt and how much cleavage to show or not to show. How was I ever going to get naked with some guy who hadn't been there over the years witnessing the gradual slide from eighteen-year-old perfection? My ex-husband, bless his heart, knew the flaws of my thirty-eight-year-old body—the weight gains and losses, the pregnancy stretch marks. Who would want the barely bouncy breasts that once bounced like beach balls until nursing stole their perk? Plastic surgery is looking pretty darn good, but until then, I work out and decided to do the best I can with the body I have now!

If you've been in a long marriage or relationship, you've likely had some of the same thoughts. We've already talked about all the women who lose a long-term partner and never date again. Dating—online or other-wise—makes them too nervous. They let fear and negativity keep them from getting the kind of relationship they want. But it doesn't have to be this way.

Every success in my life started with acting *as if*. The first time I auditioned for a part in a community theater, I pretended to be a famous actress doing a monologue. I got the part, and I was only twelve years old. When I started my first company, I acted as if I understood how to invest in real estate until the time came when I actually did. When I had my daughter, I went about parenting as if I knew what to do with a child. Over time, as my confidence grew, I realized I could do a pretty darn good job raising my daughter. When I wrote my first book and became a professional speaker, I acted as if I'd been speaking about social media for years, and in that first talk in front of thirty people, I sounded like a pro. Now I have a successful company serving clients all over the world, and I speak to groups of three hundred without batting an eye. It all started with acting *as if*, the key to my success and my happiness, and my FAE helps me pull it off.

With online dating, an FAE and acting *as if* will get you over the fear hump. What if your body had gorgeous qualities you've forgotten about? What if you were brave enough to go after the men you desired? What if dating and flirting were a piece of cake for you? OK maybe they aren't that easy for you, but these things are very easy for your Fearless Alter Ego.

Beyonce's Sasha Fierce helped her conquer her stage fright. Now let's create your Sasha Fierce or Fearless Alter Ego name. It's simple. Take the first name of your favorite doll or stuffed animal from childhood plus the last word of your favorite handbag or shoe brand. For example,

my favorite doll's name was Abigail. She was my favorite even though I wasn't a huge fan of dolls, and I often left her on the driveway naked in the rain. My favorite brand of shoes is Jimmy Choos. I don't own a pair yet, but hopefully this book will be so wildly successful that I'll own several by the time you're reading this. My Fearless Alter Ego is Abigail Choo. Sexy, isn't it?

26

You're going to need your Fearless Alter Ego a lot to manage this online dating world, especially at first. When you want to chicken out on something that will lead you to what you want, don't. Hand it over to your alter ego and keep moving. Ask yourself what she would do. Your FAE is gorgeous, brilliant, sexy, and confident. She's all the good parts of you put together and on display for the world to see. She's honest about what she wants and takes the necessary steps to move forward.

Test this theory today by taking one little step. If there's a cute guy you've been eyeing at the coffee house, let your FAE tell him hello. If you typically wear turtlenecks up to your chin like a nun, let your FAE show the tiniest bit of cleavage. If you have no idea what you would say on an online dating profile, let your FAE write down all those things that are downright fabulous about you.

This might seem like a silly game. Great! Who knew that improving your life could be so much fun? Over time, however, the playacting brings about real change. One day you'll find you've accidentally adopted behaviors that enable you to take control of your life and move toward what you want. First act *as if*, and then watch true fearlessness become who you are.

Chapter 6

Forty Million People Can't All Be Wrong: The Case for Online Dating

I've heard all the objections to online dating. I'm sure you have too. They've probably stopped you from trying it for yourself.

- *I want to meet someone organically.* (Right. Like at the fruit stand, maybe?)

- *I'd rather meet someone in person.* (If you've had luck with that, more power to you, but the odds are against you.)

- *The online dating world is full of freaks.* (Yes. The *world* is full of freaks.)

- *Most of the dating sites are just for booty calls.* (Not true. But what's wrong with a booty call now and then?)

- *Online dating is for losers.* (Do I sound like a loser to you? You don't seem like a loser to me. Your taste in books is obviously impeccable.)

Let's look at the numbers. You can see more of the online dating research results at the back of this book. For the moment, focus on these stats. It doesn't take a math wiz to see that online dating is here to stay.

Online dating has grown to become a billion dollar industry. Rates vary by website, but on average, according to StatisticBrain.com, an American will spend $239 a year on online dating. This survey indicates that more than forty million of the fifty-eight million single Americans log on to find love. Americans in their mid-twenties to mid-forties, the largest online dating demographic, have turned to dating sites instead of looking to meet someone at a bar or restaurant, where, according to Match.com, only 9 percent of women and 2 percent of men luck into love.

A study by the National Academy of Sciences suggests online dating has not only changed the way relationships begin, but it has also increased overall marital happiness and longevity. These statistics show that today more than one-third of marriages begin online. The industry has grown in strides since 2005, with almost double the amount of Americans finding a long-lasting relationship on an online dating site, according to Pew Research Center.

Before you race to the computer, let this little tidbit sink in. The world of dating, both online and offline, operates in men's favor. Match.com's research indicates that for every eighty-six unmarried men there are one hundred unmarried women, so it's a competitive game for us. Not that we're going to let that stop us. It just means you were damn smart to buy this book so you can outsmart all those other chicks.

First, let's address some of the objections people have to online dating.

I want to meet someone organically.

Hey, I hear you. Here's how it happens to me in my romantic dreams. I'm sitting in a coffeehouse having a perfect hair day, looking about thirty pounds lighter. I'm sipping a vanilla latte with whipped cream when a tall, dark, and handsome gentleman walks in the door. Our eyes lock. A sly smile spreads across his face. He's wearing tight jeans and a tighter t-shirt. His hair is lusciously wavy. He walks over to me and says, "Hi. You have some whipped cream on your lips that looks endearingly silly. I'm going to buy a latte with whipped cream too, and I'll come sit next to you and get some whipped cream on my lips so you won't be the only silly one in the room." I hike up my dropped jaw and watch him saunter up to the counter. We spend the next three hours talking and laughing. Then he asks for my number. He walks me to my car and leans me against the front fender. His strong, calloused hand braces my neck as he kisses the remaining cream off my lips.

This has yet to happen even though I spend a hell of a lot of time in coffeehouses. Sure an organic meeting would be the stuff of dreams, but if you're living in the real world, you've probably noticed that strangers have become less inclined to approach each other in person. I'm not saying it doesn't happen. But I wouldn't hold my breath.

If you give online dating a shot, you still have the same chance of meeting someone more organically, so what do you have to lose?

The online dating world is full of freaks.

I agree with you on this one, and I've got plenty of stories to tell to support your point of view. For instance, my friend Julia met a guy online, and the conversation was going great. Eventually he asked her out. His idea for a first date was quite intriguing. He suggested they go shoe shopping. Julia thought it was a joke and laughed, but he explained his strong desire to see, touch, and smell her feet. She decided even though Cinderella had gotten her man with a shoe, she was going to pass.

My friend Mallory decided to give online dating a shot, and right off the bat she started chatting with an attractive fellow who said he was a doctor. Woo hoo! She googled him, and sure enough, he was a well-known surgeon and a high-profile socialite. He asked Mallory on a first date, offering to pick her up at her house like an old-fashioned gentleman. (You should never let a first date pick you up at your house, but we'll discuss that later.) Mallory invited him in and offered him a glass of wine (another online dating don't). When she got back from the kitchen with his glass of wine, Doc was on the couch with his pants down around his knees, and he was stroking something that wasn't the English bulldog sitting next to him. Mallory's look of shock sent him packing, and she never saw him again, except in the social section of the newspaper where it was difficult to recognize him with his pants on.

Yes, like Julia, Mallory—and me—you'll run into some freaks. But here's the truth. The world in general is full of freaks, and dating online gives you a better shot at sifting through them more quickly and easily. You should appreciate the increased efficiency.

Most of the online dating sites are for booty calls.
There are many sites, and many people on dating sites who are looking for booty calls, but not all of the sites or all of the people are all about booty. (Hey that might be your goal here; I'm not one to judge.) Different sites are designed for different types of relationships. (We'll cover this topic in chapter nine.)

People have certain goals in mind when they date online or offline, and some people are just looking for sex. Online dating doesn't change these goals. Online dating just makes the goal more obvious. For example, if you meet a guy in a bar, he probably won't say right off the bat, "Hey, I just want to bang. I'm not interested in seeing you after tonight," although that may well be his intention. If you were meeting online, the same guy would likely indicate that he just wants to hang out and isn't looking for a relationship. This is valuable information that makes your decisions on who to date much more efficient.

Online dating is for losers.
I certainly hope this isn't true because it would mean I'm a loser and don't know it. I've met many successful, brilliant women who do online dating, and I've met and dated attractive, wealthy men thanks to online sites. I've certainly met some losers dating online but not nearly as many

as you might think. I've also met plenty of losers dating offline. I don't think the ratio is different in the real world, and online dating enables us to sift through the losers and winners more quickly.

I chose online dating because, going into a relationship, I like knowing the goal of the person I may date. Thanks to a busy career and the daughter I'm raising with my ex-husband, I'm limited on time. Most nights, when I have her, I'm at home with her. I'm not out at bars or clubs meeting available men, and I'm pretty sure that men my age aren't swarming bars either. Like me, they're probably busy with their careers and home with their kids part of the time. On the nights I don't have my daughter, I want to be on a date, not searching for someone to date.

Times have changed. Technology has entered every area of our lives. Why not use it to change your life for the better?

Chapter 7

It's All about Perspective:
Don't Stand Next to Angelina Jolie

I went to a singles mixer at a posh Dallas hotel a while back. I was pretty pumped about paying a few bucks to get into an event full of single men. Unfortunately, I'd forgotten there would be all these other single women showing up. Damn. Who had to go and invite them?

Let me explain. I'm in Dallas, and most of the women who live here are gorgeous. The typical Dallas woman is thin, dressed to the nines, and sporting designer handbags and shoes that are more expensive than my entire outfit. I'm not jealous—heck, I admire their style. I've got big boobs and a small sense of style. At a live dating event, those skinny, well-dressed women are my competition, and they're hard to beat.

I attended this singles mixer with my friend Maria and six of her girlfriends. Four of us worked our way through a gaggle of posh singles and headed out to the pool to sample the margaritas. By the time I reached the poolside bar, I was alone and confused. What the heck just happened? I turned to scan the crowd. There they were, like a trail of bread crumbs dropped along the way. Each one of them had been picked up—in under two minutes!

Instead of listening to the air hiss out of my balloon, I took the opportunity to analyze the situation. Acquaintance number one, a well-dressed, thin, pretty, Asian woman, had been picked up by a not-so-attractive guy, but heck at least she got picked up. Acquaintance number two, another well-dressed, thin, pretty, Asian woman, was talking to a handsome, young buck. Acquaintance number three—you guessed it. Asian. Pretty. Thin. Check, check, check.

Am I saying that Asian women are inherently more desirable than white women? Nope, I'm not. Um, at least I don't think I am. What I am saying is that you have to pay attention to perspective and the games it plays on the mind.

Standing alone, I'm a cute, voluptuous, white woman with wild, curly, blonde hair. Standing next to those three svelte Asian girls, I'm a heifer. Perspective is a bitch. Let's not forget, though, that the right guy, who likes exactly what I'm working with, could see me standing next to a hundred hot Asian chicks and still walk right up and ask for my number.

I'm not suggesting you dump all of your skinny, hot friends. You just might not want to stand next to them at the bar while attempting to get picked up. You don't need ugly friends to stand next to either. You just need to understand that some nights and in some guys' eyes you're going to be the best looking woman in the place, and sometimes you aren't. Embrace the concept of perspective, and deal with it.

Let's start with what guys are going to notice first—the physical.

If you don't know what amazing physical gifts you've brought to the world, how do you expect guys to? You've lived in your body your whole life, but have you taken the time to get to know it and appreciate it? Find ways to accentuate the positive.

Right now, stop and ask another person, preferably a dude, what your best physical attributes are. If you're alone, go check yourself out in the mirror. Write down four physical attributes that you or your friend like about your appearance. Mine, for example, are hair, boobs, legs, eyes.

I don't want to hear about your sparkling personality here. This is strictly physical. And I don't want to hear any negative talk like, "Oh, no, look at my big stomach. How can anyone see anything good on my body when that's there?" Squash those negative thoughts immediately and focus on the positive. You wouldn't let another person speak to you that way, so don't take that smack from yourself.

Worth noting: When perspective plays games with your mind, remember perspective comes into play on the guy's end too. You'd be wise to remember this when you receive your first dick pic. Unless that thing is next to a Coke can, don't get too excited. Oh, and don't forget, Coke cans now come in those little half sizes.

Chapter 8

Widening Your Horizons: Italian Men Are the Best Lovers And Other Stereotypes

I'm traveling alone, sitting on a plane full of strangers, heading for a week in Umbria, where I'll be staying at a villa taking cooking lessons. This is quite laughable because, essentially, I don't cook. In my life, I'm either amazingly fantastic at something or dreadfully horrible, and this battle of extremes applies as much to my cooking as everything else. Every time I try out a new recipe it's either instantly addicting or completely inedible. Worse, the ratio is about one to five.

I could tell you that I'm going to Italy for the cooking lessons, which theoretically I am. Or I could say that I'm going to Italy to have solitary time to focus on writing this book. Once again that would be a true statement. I could also explain to you that I'm going to Italy to make over my soul, train for an upcoming half marathon, or learn more about drinking Moscato. All true. But the real reason I'm going to Italy is Al Pacino.

No, sadly, Al isn't meeting me for a secret love affair. But the image of Al Pacino in *The Godfather* movies is burned into my memory. As a young girl watching him, I formed my ideal man—handsome, strong, and desirable. It never occurred to me that gangsters probably weren't ideal mates or husbands. No, this was naïve, raw, sexual attraction. Italian men became my thing the day I saw Michael Corleone take Apollonia in his arms.

I was so fascinated with Italian men that I was determined to date one. I loved their dark eyes, dark hair, dark skin. My pulse raced at the sound of the language, the drama, and even the yelling. I'd heard they were amazing lovers, and I wanted to find out for myself. Unfortunately, I lived in Louisiana, then Texas, and there just weren't that many Italian men around. I ended up marrying a tall, white guy from Mesquite, Texas, and we all know how that ended.

Decades later, newly divorced at age thirty-nine, I decided to go to Italy and find out what all the fuss is about.

Is there a type of man you've always been attracted to or curious about? I'm not talking about your fascination with guys who are assholes, if that's what comes to mind. That last relationship didn't work out, so obviously it's time to do something different.

This is your chance. You're single, and it's time to see what you've been missing. If you don't explore, you'll never know who's waiting for you just around the bend. It's all part of educating yourself, making an informed decision about the person you choose for your next relationship.

Sometimes it's the unexpected that kicks us right in the gut in a very good way. When I began dating, I stuck with guys who were just a little bit older. When I finally agreed to go out with someone much younger, it was thrilling to see how much fun it could be (more juicy details on the young guy later). I always dated men who were physically fit, but one day I decided to follow up with a nerdy, slightly overweight, out-of-shape guy. To my surprise, I was attracted to him. His body felt delicious, and I thought, *hey, maybe this is what guys think when they feel my body in their arms*. Quite frankly, this was an excellent thought.

We are so programmed by what society says is the perfect, desirable body that we forget to stop and ask what we truly desire. Perhaps we yearn for something other than the hard abs, the full head of hair, and the tall drink of water in the ads. Entertain the possibility of enjoying the unexpected. In the end, it's all about what sets your heart on fire.

As I'm sure you've noticed, attraction goes deeper than the physical. Consider a prospective date's personality and profession too. If you've been dating quiet doctors and you've been unhappy, then try something new—like a brooding artist or a burly fireman.

Don't let yourself stay stuck in a rut, dating the same type of guy over and over. The definition of insanity is doing the same thing repeatedly and expecting a different result. Stop that!

Get yourself a journal and do some important homework. Describe the men you've dated in the past—their physical characteristics, their personalities, their professions, and their interests. When you've written it all down, look for patterns and gain valuable insights into what has worked and what hasn't. Next think about the kind of men you'd like to date. How are they different?

Yes, it's going to take a little time and effort. But why not give it a shot? Do it now.

You may be wondering how that trip to Italy worked out for me. Let me just say, before you book your trip to Italy to find out if Italian men are good lovers, make sure to check the Groupon you bought, or you might end up staying in a remote city on top of a mountain in Umbria, where there are no more than ten men in the entire town, and they're all taken, eighty years old, or both. Plus all the guys in your group might happen to be fellow Americans at least twenty-five years older than you and gay or married.

Hey, wait a minute. I'm in Rome tonight having a dinner alone in my fancy hotel restaurant, and this very handsome waiter is being particularly attentive. Hmm.

Chapter 9

The Dating Site Dilemma:
So Many Choices. So Little Time.

You've identified your goal by nailing down your online dating personality and given some thought to past relationships: the types of guys you've dated (or married) and what kind of exploration you'd like to do. Now it's time to select where you'll do your hunting.

There are mainstream dating sites and specialty dating sites. The specialty dating sites cater to an amazing variety of tastes, including but not limited to the following:

- Plus size
- Jewish
- Christian
- Over Fifty
- Casual Sex

- Fetish
- Herpes
- Geographic Areas
- Fitness
- Single Parents

There are tons of dating sites, and they come and go. eHarmony leads the pack with more than 20 million members, followed closely by Match.com with 17 million, at least according to a study by the Proceedings of the National Academy of Sciences of the United States. I've listed them and forty-eight others in the back of this book along with a short description of what you can expect to get out of each site. You can also get an up-to-date list at www.GetItGirlGuide.com along with feedback from other women like you.

I suggest beginning with just one site. You may or may not start getting messages right away. You can tweak your profile to see if it changes your results, and you can try reaching out to guys with different messages to see what kind of response you get.

After a while, you can start adding more sites. It's important to understand that you may have no luck on one site and lots of interaction on another. This happened to me often. Success varies from site to site for different women with different goals. This is good news because we're not all looking for the same kind of men, so be patient.

There are paid and unpaid dating sites and lots of options within both. I've used both, and the unpaid sites happen to work better for me. A friend of mine had almost no luck on unpaid sites and likes only the sites that she pays for. Some free sites offer ways to upgrade to improve your results. Other sites are free to sign up on, but if you want to communicate with anybody, you have to pay a monthly fee. If money is a concern, you can get away with sticking to free sites. If you decide to pay for an upgrade later, be sure to read the fine print to learn what the fee actually gets you.

Paid sites typically have less advertising than the free sites, which make their money by having a lot of traffic and selling ad space. If you would like to save money on a paid site, there are options to sign up for longer periods of time, like three or six months, for a discounted rate. Always start with one month to see if you like the site, then you can choose to do a longer subscription. If many subscription options are offered, always start with the lowest-cost version. You can increase your spending if you find there are options you truly cannot live without.

I've found that after successfully using a particular dating site for three or four months, I often hit a lull. If you send out lots of messages and find that nothing is working, my advice is to consider deleting your account completely. I call this the shiny and new method. Wait about sixty days, then open a new account with a new username and, ideally, new pics. Your write-up can be identical or changed slightly. The important thing is men will see you as new to the site. It's like a little refresh. You can keep your dates up by rotating when you purge, restarting periodically on a variety of sites.

Is your head spinning? No worries. Next we're going to work on your brand—yes, you're marketing yourself—and your online dating profile.

Chapter 10

Going Live:
The Nuts and Bolts of Online Dating

The two most important building blocks of your online dating presence are your Dating Personality (Banger, Knotter, Chatter, and so on) and your Dating Brand. Remember, online dating is like eBay for humans. If you don't promote yourself, you'll get lost in a sea of thirty-nine-year-old, white, divorced moms.

First you need a USP—a Unique Selling Proposition. In marketing, that's what they call a company's brand. Your USP is like a slogan that tells the world what sets you apart, what you offer, and what you do. Here's mine:

> "Yep, I'm cute, and I've got curves and curls. I'm a mom, an author, a speaker, and a CEO. I'm a hot-blooded woman, and I've been told I'm funny even a bit outrageous, but I've never been

called boring. I love to play drums, go bowling, and sing karaoke, even though I do all of these things badly. I want to date a wicked smart, handsome, gutsy man who will kiss me in elevators, spoil me, and enjoy me spoiling him back."

Not bad, right? Here's what I could have written instead:

"I'm a thirty-nine-year-old, plus-size, divorced mom who owns a company. I'm outgoing and have a good sense of humor. I want to go on nonboring dates with a good looking, smart guy who will treat me right."

After reading both of those, I'll bet you remember details from the first USP and very little from the second. Why? The second one is boring and nondescript. It might as well say, "I'm the same as a zillion other women out there, and there is really nothing exciting or special about me."

Your USP should be about fifty words max, which makes it very easy for you to remember. And it's not just for online dating. E-mail it to your friends and ask them if they know a guy who would be interested in someone like this, and—surprise!—it's you. Use it to tell your friends and family how to describe you to guys you'd like them to set you up with. When you meet a guy in a bar, at a conference, or at the grocery store, and he says, "Tell me about yourself," I want these few, perfectly crafted sentences to come out of your mouth. Your USP is your dating elevator pitch, and if you're in the market for a date, you must have one.

So let's build your USP. Go get your notebook or your computer and a coffee or a glass of wine, and we'll get through this together. Ready?

Remember in chapter seven when you took a good look at yourself and listed your top physical attributes? Rifle through your notebook and find them. If you were too chicken to write them down, you're going to have to do it now. We can't build your brand without them. It's OK. I'll wait.

That wasn't so bad, was it? Now we can get started. The USP should begin with the physical because that's where attraction begins. You rarely hear someone say, "Check her out. She looks so smart. Her brain is super hot." I agree that big brains are attractive, but that isn't discovered until after a physical attraction inspires two people to start talking in the first place.

Your online pictures will do most of the work for you, but you shouldn't leave that initial attraction to chance. Make sure he noticed. With a little creativity, you might even inspire him to take a second look. So write a short sentence about your physical attributes. They don't all have to be in the sentence, and for heaven's sake, don't make it sound like a grocery list. Be as subtle or as naughty as you wish, depending on your personality, and keep your Dating Personality in mind. Show him that you're self-aware and confident.

For example, my top physical attributes are my hair, boobs, legs, face, eyes, and butt. However, I'm not going to leave it at that. I get the point across in a much more memorable way by saying, "Yep, I'm cute and I've got curls and curves." I'm hoping to show that I'm confident, casual, and aware of my nice body parts.

Here are some more ideas to get you started.

The Facts	The Spin
You have a great butt.	You'll hate to see me leave, but you'll enjoy watching me walk away.
You have great hair and legs.	If you like dark hair that feels like silk and long legs that come up to my neck, I'm for you.
You have soft skin and blue eyes.	I've got skin as smooth as porcelain and eyes the color of the sea.

Now it's your turn. Conduct a brainstorming session. Gather all keywords, phrases, slogans, positioning statements, and other people's descriptions of you, and jot them on a white board or yellow pad. Dissect, distill, discuss with friends, create a survey and send it out if you have to. At this point, you're just looking for bullet points. Keep it simple.

Once you've done your due diligence, draw on your research to answer each of the following questions creatively. Write a short sentence in three versions for each, and then circle your favorites.

- What are your top physical attributes? Remember, no lists!
- Who are you? Write down the first few things that come to mind—the things that make you, you.
- What do others say about you? Naturally, you're going to make it something nice or interesting.
- What hobbies or activities do you enjoy?
- What is your goal, and what kind of man do you want? The goal is Dating Personality label (Dater, Banger, Knotter).

Combine all these statements, in the same order and craft your Unique Selling Proposition (USP). Let's review: physical attributes + who you are + hobbies + dating personality + man you want = USP.

Everything is based on your USP. Use it whenever someone wants to know about you in thirty seconds or less, including, of course, your online dating profiles. When you need to create your profile summary, start with your USP and expand on it. Beyond your dating sites, social media is a great way to build awareness of your brand. Use the USP you've already created and share it on Facebook, and pull a line from it for Twitter. In real life, when a guy crosses the room to make your acquaintance, you'll never be tongue-tied again. You've got your USP!

Setting Up Your Profile

A friend of mine named Nick chatted online with a woman named Jenny. She seemed intelligent, witty, and charming. Her pictures were pretty hot too. Nick and Jenny finally decided to meet. He was sitting at the bar waiting for her when a rather mature, matronly looking woman leaning on a walker came up to him and said hello. It took a moment for Nick to realize that this was his date for the evening.

Nick tried to keep a straight face as this nice lady with freshly dyed hair, which had clearly been set in old-lady curls, asked him to order her a Tom Collins. He thought back to her profile pictures, which had obviously been taken at least twenty years earlier. Over the course of the evening, he was surprised at how much he enjoyed their conversation. He found her quite endearing, like a favorite aunt.

At the end of the evening, Nick helped Jenny to her car and loaded the walker for her. She paused before getting in the driver's seat and raised her head, crimson lips pursed, ready for a kiss that never came. Instead he politely shook her hand and helped her into her pink Caddy before she peeled out into the sunset.

The moral of the story is tell the truth. You'll be tempted to fudge some facts on your profile, but sure as the sun rising in the east, you're going to get busted. If you can't do it by yourself, channel your FAE, who knows all that's true and great about you and build that profile.

Setting up your profile is a little bit different on every site, but here are some general guidelines and rules to follow.

E-mail Address

You'll be asked to use an e-mail address to set up your account. Use your personal—not your work—e-mail address. Correspondence from the site will be coming to your e-mail, but don't worry; your address will be kept private from the men you communicate with on the dating site as long as you respond to them through the site's inbox.

Username

It would be great to have a cute username, but so many are already taken by other creative gals like you that you'll need to think for a bit on this one. You want something easy to remember, and it shouldn't be something that gives a guy the wrong idea. Think about your dating personality and go from there. If you're a Knotter looking for a serious relationship, don't choose a username that makes you sound like an eager Banger. GoDownOnYou or BigBoobsNeedFun won't attract much marriage material.

Many people pick usernames that include their year of birth, like SoccerChick74 or Librarian65. This is fine, but I'm not a huge fan. What if your prospects get confused and think you're a seventy-four-year-old soccer chick? It could happen. Never use your year of birth if you were born in 1969. Guys' minds light up for all the wrong reasons.

Privacy

I 'm not a fan of including first names in the username or anywhere in the profile for that matter. You can exchange first names during your first or second conversation. Don't reveal your last name until you've decided to meet the person, or even later. Unless you work at a very large company, don't reveal where you work until you're comfortable with the idea of this person being able to track you down. Don't ever give out your home or work address. When asked where you live, you simply give the city or the area. And of course, never give bank account information or password information no matter how many times a guy whines about getting detained in a foreign country. Scams like this happen rarely, but they do happen, so be smart.

Where You Live

Indicate your zip (or postal) code or town so the site can help you identify targets that are close to you. If you live in two areas, choose the area you live in most of the time or the area you prefer to do most of your dating in.

Year of Birth

I know it's tough for some of you, but every site is going to ask for your birth date, including the year. Once you enter it, you won't be able to change it. Period. I'm going to encourage you to go ahead, suck it up, and just tell the truth. Age is a fact of life. We can't change it, and everyone around us is getting older too. This is one of those times I don't recommend acting *as if*. Act your age.

Relationship Status

Tell the truth—single, divorced, separated, or married—and hope that your suitors will too. If you're separated but soon to be divorced, choose separated in the relationship status, and state when you expect to be divorced in your summary section. Some suitors will pass you by until you're divorced. Others won't think it's a big deal. You might be put off or confused by people who indicate they're married. What the heck are they doing on a dating site? They're either looking for someone on the sly, or they're in an open marriage. Two terms I learned doing online dating are *polyamorous* and *polyamory*. They refer to people who are open to engaging in multiple relationships simultaneously.

Height

Men are more guilty of lying on this one than women. Once again, my suggestion is to tell the truth. The hope is that you're actually going to meet someone, and you don't want to have to explain why you're six inches taller or shorter than you said you were on the site.

Body Type

This is the one most women abhor. I know I do. Guys will often use this search to filter out the physical characteristics they don't find desirable. The trick is to tell the truth. That way the men who are looking for you can find you, and the ones who won't dig you, don't. Problems arise when the selections include descriptions like *BBW (Big, Beautiful Woman)*, *Full Figured*, *Curvy*, *A Few Extra Pounds*, *Average*, *Athletic*, *Skinny*. Bite the bullet and choose the selection that corresponds best to your type. Ask your girlfriends for their opinions. You might do a search for ten or more women on that particular site with bodies similar to yours. It doesn't mean their label is right—they're probably guessing just like you—but it might give you an idea of how others see themselves. At first I was choosing *Full Figured*, and my results weren't very good. Then my girlfriend told me she thought I was more in the *A Few Extra Pounds* category. Sure enough, when I switched to this, my interactions increased.

Hair and Eye Color

Choose the closest matches, and if you change your hair color, remember to change it on the dating site too.

Looking for

Indicate you're looking for men, women, or both. Be sure to choose, or you may be surprised to find notes from suitors that you're not interested in.

Income

Either leave this blank or fill it out and select "do not reveal." Why? If you met a guy in a bar or through friends, you wouldn't walk up to him and say, "Hi, my name is Samantha. I'm a VP of Sales, and I make $95,000 a year." No. That would be weird. Don't list your income publicly in any situation. If you don't make much money, you might be judged for that and passed by. If you make lots of money, you might be targeted as a sugar mama. This information should be private until you're ready to share.

Religion

Once again, it's important to be honest and choose the selection that most closely matches your belief system. This is especially important if you will only date a partner who is the same religion as you.

Relationship selection

Here you state your goal—the one you identified in chapter two.

Your Dating Personality

Feel free to make more than one selection here if it's allowed. Choices will include *Friends*, *Hang out*, *Casual*

Sex, Short-term Dating, Long-term Dating, Long-term Relationship, etc. If you can select only one, choose the one you want most of all. For example, if you're open to casual sex but really want a long-term relationship, select *Long-term Relationship.* If your only selection is *Casual Sex*, make sure you're a pure banger because some men who are looking for someone to go out on dates will filter you out of their search. Selecting *Casual Sex* will ensure plenty of prospects, but you should be ready for the barrage of dirty talk and naked pictures that will fill up your dating-site inbox.

Hang out is a bit of a confusing term, as some people think it means casual dating while others expect banging and no date. I would suggest staying away from selecting *Hang out* unless you feel it really explains your goal. *Activity Partner* is another term with varying definitions. Some take it to mean they're seeking a person to do things but not to date, and others see it as a way to find someone whom they might eventually date. I stay away from this selection as well since I think the intention is murky.

Politics

Select the option that matches your views most closely.

Interests

Dating sites are powered by search engines, so the more interests you list here the better. If you say you like sky-diving and sushi, men who like these things will find you more easily and vice versa. Think about all your hobbies, talents, and activities and fill out this section with single words or short phrases, not complete sentences.

Summary

Start with your USP and expand on it. Keep it at three or four short paragraphs. You don't want summaries to be too short because guys won't learn enough about you, and you don't want to go on and on because they'll think, jeez, this girl never shuts up.

Chapter 11

Get Ready for Your Closeup:
The Dreaded Profile Pics

When I started dating online, I put three pictures of myself up on the dating site and wrote an engaging, humorous, and adorable profile. Were men enthralled by my witty writing and swarming to get a chance to talk to this big, beautiful brain? Nope. Although I had a few nibbles, my results were dismal.

One afternoon during a deep exploration of my bed-room closet, my friend Maria put together an outfit for me—a black leather skirt that hit just above the knee, red, peep-toe heels, and a black shirt that showed the tiniest hint of cleavage. Maria demanded I work it for the camera, and she snapped a picture which, amazingly, I did not hate.

I added that image to my profile, though my results had been so low I really didn't see how one picture could make much of a difference. The next morning I logged in, and what the hell? I had eleven messages in my inbox! Does one little picture make that much difference? The answer is yes. It does.

Most men are highly visual creatures, and profile pictures are your bait. Consequently, they're the most important part of your profile. Your pictures should look like the best version of you. Not the version twenty years or twenty pounds ago, but the version of you within the last six months or six pounds. You don't want to show up on a date and hear, "Who the hell are you?" One of the best lines on a guy's online dating profile I've ever seen was, "If we meet and you don't look like your profile pictures, you'll be buying me drinks until you do!"

In a perfect world, you should have some guy friends give you their feedback on your pictures, but if there are no guys available, ask your girlfriends. The reactions you're going for should be something like this:

"You look great!"

"You look pretty!"

"You look hot!"

What you don't want to hear is this:

"Who is that?"

"Is that your daughter?"

"Is that your nipple?"

You're going to need a minimum of three pictures, and they need to be in a specific order, so let's review.

The Main Shot

The main shot is the one that shows up first when you communicate with someone on an online dating site. It should be a headshot, and you should be smiling, not looking like you're on antidepressants—unless you're a Goth chick, in which case you should look pissed as hell and double up on the black lipstick and eyeliner.

In the main picture, you're showing off your most important asset—your face. You should be having a great hair day, and your makeup should accentuate your best features. I usually just wear lipstick, but for a photograph, I add foundation and blush.

The frame of the picture should go from the top of your head down to your chest. You can include your chest if you want to. It can't hurt. If you're wearing something strapless, don't crop the picture above the top edge or you'll look like you're naked and super slutty—unless you're going for super slutty. Then, by all means, employ this technique.

The Full-length Shot

Your second shot is a full-length body shot. No exceptions! No, you cannot wait until you lose more weight or you have lipo or a tummy tuck or a boob job. You need a head-to-toe picture in something that shows off your curves. If you're adventurous, fit, and proud of your body, and you want to rock a bikini or bathing suit, feel free. If you're not, find an outfit that shows off your shape, but choose one you feel good in.

You can't get away with wearing something loose in this picture. Why? Men want to see if you're dating material. In fact, many men will not reach out to women whose dating profiles show only a headshot or the top half of her body for fear that the bottom half is a size one hundred.

The outfit should be something you actually would wear on a date. If you're a sexy dresser, dress that way. If you're a conservative dresser, stick with that. In any case, the outfit should show off the shape of your body very clearly. Slimming colors are great, and proper undergarments can go a long way in helping you look your best.

In an ideal world, you'd update these pictures every three months, but that might not be realistic. However, it's imperative that you update these pictures at least every six months to increase your results. Some dating sites give you the option of rotating the pictures that show up as the main picture. I've tried this with mixed results. After one month on a site, if you have this option, try it and see if it increases the number of views or messages you receive.

The Personality Shot

In the third picture, you are building your dating brand. Go back to your USP and pick out one of the things about yourself that you like or take pride in. Pick one that's easily conveyed in a picture. For example, I'm silly, and I can make people laugh. My third picture is of me in a club wearing huge, oversized sunglasses from a novelty shop making a sexy face and rocking a great hair day. The picture is funny, but it doesn't hurt that I still look darn cute. What is it you want people to know about you?

Your personality shot might include any of the following or something entirely different:

1. **Working out**—These are great because you're in figure-hugging clothes, and they show you care about taking care of your body.

2. **With your pet**

3. **With your child**—People have very mixed feelings about including their children in a dating-site picture. Some feel this puts the child's privacy at risk. Others think it shows their child is going to be around and is a priority. You need to make your own judgment call here.

4. **On vacation**

5. **Engaging in your hobby**

6. **At work**

7. **With friends**—This is a tricky one. In group pictures, sometimes it's hard to tell which one you are. Sometimes our friends look hotter than we do. Do we really want them standing next to us in a picture on a dating site? I don't think so. I've heard stories from women who had pictures of themselves with friends on dating sites, and men asked if they could meet one of the friends. Don't risk it—crop friends out. If it's a guy friend with you in the shot, some men will think that's your boyfriend and you're looking for a third party to join them in the bedroom. Even if it's your dad and you write in the caption, "My dad and I," some guys will think you're with this older man. I say leave everybody but you on the cutting room floor.

All the profile pictures beyond the third are extras, and the more you have, the better your chances of getting a response. Some data suggests that women with more than ten pictures on their dating profiles receive eight times more messages. However, I'm inclined to max it out at ten shots so you look like you have a life other than uploading your mug on dating sites. For your extra shots, use any of the Personality Picture ideas. Any image that shows you looking particularly lovely will do.

Once you get to the texting stage with a man, one of the first things he will probably ask you for is a picture. This request should be a cute, smiling picture of you that does not appear anywhere on your dating profile. Ideally, it would be a picture you snap yourself right when he requests it, but if you look like crap at that moment, use one you already have on your phone. Why is he asking for this photo? Probably so he can save it with your contact info on his phone. That way when he texts you, he doesn't get you mixed up with the six other women he's chatting with that he met online. You should do the same and save his picture in your phone because this book is going to make you so good at online dating you'll be getting to the texting stage with multiple guys at the same time, and the last thing you want to do is think you're flirting with twenty-five-year-old social media pro Sam when you're really texting with forty-two-year-old Julian the Pastor.

For all your photos, consider yourself warned: Don't take pictures that don't match who you are or what you are trying to accomplish! If you're a vegetarian against gun ownership, don't post a picture of you dove hunting. If you go out drinking once a year and would prefer a man who rarely drinks as well, don't post a picture of you doing shots. If you go to church every Sunday and wear shirts that are buttoned up to your neck, don't post the pic of that one time you went to Rio and danced in a bikini at Carnivale. In other words, be real. Truth in advertising gets you guys who choose the real you.

Make sure your photographer is a trusted friend. They have to be patient, willing to take tons of pictures in different lighting, outfits, and positions to come up with a few you'll like. I know it's tough. Most of us hate having our pictures taken. But have some fun with it. Bring out your Fearless Alter Ego and let her rock the pics. Watch an episode of *America's Next Top Model* before you begin, and Google Tyra's lessons on smizing and the all-important booty tooch.

I'm picturing you now, and you look fabulous!

Chapter 12

Truth or Dare:
Deciphering His Profile

I showed my friend Brisa a picture of Brian, a tall, thirty-two-year-old. To say he was built would be an understatement. Brisa took a two-second gander. "Don't do it!"

"Why not?" I asked.

"He's on steroids! Look at his body. He works out too much, and you know what that means."

No actually, I didn't know. I'd heard rumors, but when I don't investigate things myself, I tend not to believe them. So, like an idiot, I exchanged a few sentences with him online, and he asked for my number. I should have read his first date description, but I was being lazy. Take this as a warning: Always read everything on your prospect's profile. Every last word!

Our first phone conversation left my mouth hanging open. It went something like this:

> **Brian:** "Hey Sexy, it's Brian. Are you ready for some fun?"
>
> **Me:** "Uh, hi Brian. I think so. Do you want to meet for a drink?"
>
> **Brian:** "Did you not read my profile? There's no drink. I've wasted too much money on women who aren't what they say they are. I've been doing online dating for years, and I'm going to tell you how I do it. You and I are going to meet, and we're going to have some fun."
>
> **Me:** "Fun?"
>
> **Brian:** "Yes. Fun. Do I need to spell it out for you? S-E-X. My house or yours?"

I started laughing because I thought he was joking, but oh, no, this was no joke, and he was pissed.

> **Brian:** (Yelling now) "Why are you laughing?"
>
> **Me:** "Sorry." (getting control of myself) "I thought you were joking. So, Brian, let me get this straight. We can't have coffee or a drink together first? I have to go to your house, say hello, and immediately bang you? How would I know I would be safe? Maybe you're a killer."

Brian: "Well, I'm not a killer, obviously. You can ask anyone I know, and they're all still alive." (Brilliant deduction)

Me: "How would I know I want to bang you if I haven't even met you?"

Brian: "Listen, girlie. I think you need to go back and look at my pictures again. If you don't know you want to bang me, you have some mental issues." (Fascinating how people with mental issues often accuse the people around them of being freaks.)

Me: "Well, Brian, call me crazy, but I like to have a conversation with someone before I bang him."

Brian: "Why?"

Me: "I prefer to have sex with smart people."

Brian: "Smart? Are you saying I'm not smart? I have a freaking bachelor's degree."

Me: "That really makes me laugh. Have you met some of the people with a bachelor's degree? I'm pretty sure that a degree does not guarantee intelligence."

Brian: "Apparently you don't understand who you're dealing with. If we f—k, a whole new world will open up to you. You will be amazed.

After that, I'll take you out on dates, but there's no way I'm spending money on you before I get you in the sack."

Me: "No problem. How about we meet for a drink, and I pay for my own?" (At this point, I have got to meet this person and see that he is real.)

Brian: "I am a massive catch. I have dated celebrities, for God's sake! You don't understand how lucky you are to be talking to me! I don't need this shit."

Me: "I understand what you don't need, Brian, but you don't understand what I need. Would you like me to spell it out for you?"

Brian: "Forget it."

Click. I resisted the urge to call him back and ask for a list of his celebrity hookups, but I just had to send him one final text.

Me: "Thanks for the entertainment."

He didn't text me back—probably busy talking to Jennifer Lopez.

If I had read Brian's profile more closely, I would never have had that conversation. Here are the highlights of Brian's description of his ideal first date:

"I'm not focused on a date right away. Now if things click, then I plan so many fun things to do. . . . You'll be smiling :) . . . . It's Dallas, so us guys have to be cautious because when women are so focused on going out to eat and going out for drinks—red flag to us! I keep things very chill and simple in the beginning."

It goes on, but you get the picture. Read a prospect's profile, and I mean *all* of his profile. Some men will talk about their love for kids, puppies, and rainbows and go on to say they can't wait to chain you up for an orgy with aliens. You have got to read it all and assume they're serious about everything they say.

Some women tend to justify statements in men's profile. The guy writes, "I'm a Republican, and I don't date Democrats, and I would prefer to never meet another Democrat for the rest of my life because they're idiots." There are women who think, oh, he's cute. He won't think I'm an idiot just because I'm a dyed-in-the-wool, yellow dog Democrat. Yes, he will! He made it very clear. Haven't you learned yet that you can't change a man—before or after you meet him?

The only time you shouldn't believe what's in his profile is when it sounds too good to be true. Chances are, it isn't, but you never know, so investigate further. Be wary of military men who say things like, "I am currently at an undisclosed location, and I can't meet anyone in person for the next month because I am in a secret government program." Believe me: the James Bonds of the world are not trolling for dates on Match.com.

Along my amazing online dating journey, I've heard stories from both men and women about people misrepresenting themselves on dating sites. I guess people want to pretend they're someone they're not, thinking they'll land someone more desirable. The problem is, the person you desire expects a totally different you to show up.

I once began chatting with a man named Thomas. In his picture, he looked sort of handsome and fit, with dark, wavy hair. In his profile, he said he was five foot ten, worked in the medical field, never married, and had no children. We chatted briefly, and in my impatient fashion, I agreed to meet him for lunch without much vetting.

I arrived at the restaurant first. A short, bald man with a beer belly walked up to my table, stopped, and stared directly at my boobs.

"Wow!" he said.

It took me a good twenty seconds to get that this was Thomas. As one of the longest half hours of my life progressed, I learned that he had been married twice and had four children with three different women. He said money was evil, and that's why he didn't have a job. Instead he depended on the government to support him. This gave him so little money he didn't have to pay the child support he owed. At this point, I started looking around for a hidden camera, thinking I was getting punked. I asked him why his profile said he worked in the medical field. His mom was disabled, he said, so he lived with her, and she paid him for taking care of her.

At the end of the date, Thomas asked me to go out with him again on a very special date where he would teach me how to play Frisbee golf. I told him that there was no need because I was a Frisbee golf pro and appeared on the cover of last month's *Frisbee Golf* magazine. He looked perplexed and said, "There is no *Frisbee Golf* magazine." Then he got this sad, puppy-dog look on his face, like I'd just kicked him or something. "I think you're lying to me," he said. Needless to say, there was not another date. People lie on dating sites for all kinds of reasons. Sometimes you won't find out until you meet them, but if you take the time to comb through a guy's entire profile with a critical eye and look at all his pictures, you'll weed out a lot of clunkers.

Chapter 13

Riddle Me This:
Decoding His Profile Pics

I once started talking to a guy who looked very cute in his main profile photo. We spoke for a few days online and decided we would meet for coffee. The night before our date, I rechecked his profile to get ready. That's when I clicked through the two additional photos. One was a side view that revealed a previously hidden, full-blown mullet! It was a mullet major too, not a mullet minor. A mullet minor could happen if someone waited just a little too long for a haircut—but no. This was a purposeful business in the front, party in the back hairstyle obviously developed with full awareness and intent.

It got worse. The next picture was another side view, but this time he had no pants or underwear on, and he showed off a glorious view of his beer belly and butt cheeks. Thank goodness he was covering up his junk with his hands. Needless to say, I cancelled the meeting. He asked why. I said I just felt I couldn't handle what he was bringing to the table. It wasn't a bad thing, though. I did have a dirty dream about pulling on Billy Ray Cyrus's mullet that night.

Here's what I've learned about guys' profile pictures after looking at tens of thousands over the past year. These are not hard and fast (that's what she said!) rules, but you might want to keep them in mind as you peruse.

If all his pictures are out of focus or he's wearing sunglasses and a hat,

- He is married.
- He is separated.
- He is in a relationship.
- He is hideous.
- He is in the witness protection program. Do you really want to move to Topeka and change your name to Bertha Julius Cartwright?

If he never smiles in any of his pictures,

- He is depressed and on Prozac.
- He is super boring.
- He has a total of three teeth, and none of them are in front.

If he wears neon orange and nothing but orange,

- He lives in Halloweentown.
- He had his color wheel done and was told his skin tone only works with orange.
- He is in prison.

If he looks like a model and is perfectly gorgeous in every picture,

- He is a model and perfectly gorgeous (unlikely but I guess it's possible).
- He found these pictures online.
- He is a Catfish.
- He is a graphic designer who is super good with Photoshop.

Pictures are a good indicator of motivation and initiative. Men who are in marketing and sales have an advantage in this area, because they realize they're marketing a product—themselves. These guys will always post more than three shots. The photos feature them doing the things they think women want them to be doing—smiling, interacting with children or puppies, playing a sport, participating in a charity, or fixing something. Images like this say that the guy has enough oomph to get up and make these pictures happen. Also he cares enough about his online dating goal to post pictures that he thinks could generate results.

When a guy posts one or two shots, it usually means he's not confident in his appearance, or he's so confident that he thinks he shouldn't have to make an effort. The shirtless pictures the guys take of themselves in the bathroom mirror are terrible no matter how hot some of the guys may be. And if you're new to this, you'll soon discover that it happens at an alarmingly high rate. Even worse, sometimes the camera angles almost capture their junk. Another fun bathroom shot includes the toilet in the background—with the seat up. There's your future with these guys! They're showing you in living color the effort they're willing to put into dating and life in general.

Men will often choose pictures that they feel say something important about them, so pay attention. I once saw a shot of a guy holding a gun bigger than him. Now I'm not against guns, but this picture communicated he was way more into guns than I'm comfortable with. If you hate outdoor activities and your prospect has a fishing shot, a camping shot, and one shot of him skinning a deer with blood smeared on his face, you might want to move on to the next guy.

If you think a guy is even remotely attractive in his main picture, take a few seconds and click on his other shots to check them out. Guys generally don't take as much time to fix themselves up and look their very best in pictures, so give him a couple of extra chances. Also always make sure you click through all of his images, or you just might end up with a beer bellied mullet head—and it won't be a young Billy Ray Cyrus.

Chapter 14

He Said What?!
The Chat Phase

Once you have your profile set up, you're going to begin receiving messages from guys saying all kinds of things. Some of the messages will be boring, offensive, or downright disgusting. You have to prepare yourself so you can enjoy this process and have a positive result. Keep in mind the messages you receive aren't really about you. They're telling you about the sender.

I've spoken to women who feel offended. They take the messages personally. But you're not going to waste your time with this attitude. Each time you receive a message via your online dating site from someone you haven't met, you can pick one of three ways to take action:

1. Delete immediately.
2. Laugh, share with your girlfriends, and then delete.
3. Investigate the sender and possibly respond.

You might as well know the truth: The majority of the time you're going to be deleting. Here's a step-by-step guide to processing a new message from a new online suitor.

> **Step 1:** Read the message. If it's offensive or gross, delete it. If the message is totally outrageous or funny, laugh and share it with your friends. Never miss the opportunity to find joy in this experience as you should in all of life's experiences.

> **Step 2:** If the message is polite but kind of boring, not bad, or somewhat intriguing, proceed to the sender's profile to investigate. If the sender's profile fits your requirements, send a message in response.

I'm sure you'd like to know what to expect, so here are a few samples of actual messages I've received. As you read these, think about your response. Would you delete or investigate the sender and possibly respond? There's no wrong answer. This is all about your preferences, not mine or anybody else's.

- "Did you just get a parking ticket because you have FINE written all over you."
- "Nice twins!" (Tip: he wasn't talking about my kids because I have only one)
- "Can I get to know you better?"
- "Hello."
- "Hi, I'm Jared. U look like maybe ur rich. U will probably take one look at my caveman ways and run for the hills. Lol. Any luck yet?"
- "Are you into younger guys?"
- "Do you date black men?"
- "Ever tried a Latino before?"
- "I wish you were punishing me so bad. I want to be your little sissy boy and do anything you say."
- "Can you handle that?" (With a shot of his junk attached—yep, very first message)
- "I like your wild hair."
- "Want to grab a drink?"
- "Want to surprise my husband with me?" (From a girl)
- "Do you like girls too?" (Also from a girl)
- "I have a wife, but I'm looking for a playmate."
- "Nice tits."

- "Hi, how have you been? Any plans for the weekend?"
- "I lost my phone number; can I have yours?"
- "Send me a dirty pic."
- "I'm not circumcised; how do you feel about that?" (Wow. This was the first message. You do have to give the guy credit for asking about my feelings though.)
- "I thought you were cute and wanted to see if you are up for a chat."
- "Spit or swaller?"
- "Nice rack."
- "Hey! Hey!! Hey!!!"
- "I'm Steven AKA Sir Giggle Ticklebottom. I be needin' a wench for fun and games."
- "Your curly hair is gorgeous. Nice curves."
- "Here is my number. Text me."

There you go. Sweet messages, boring messages, hot messages, and gross messages are all coming your way. Just remember, these messages are not really about you. Don't get stuck wondering what's in your profile that attracts this weird stuff. It isn't you. The sender is likely sending them out to plenty of other people too. You get to pick how you respond and enjoy the process along the way.

Just for the fun of it, we'd love to hear your most disgusting, outrageous, funniest, and sweetest messages. You can share them at www.GetItGirlGuide.com or www. Sextiquette.com. But please, don't share the pics. Keep those for your own enjoyment.

Chapter 15

Searching for the One:
Or More Than One

When women decide to start dating online, they usually think they know exactly what kind of guy they're looking for, and they assume they can search for him using filters. I went into this thinking I wanted a good-looking, forty-year old, CEO/entrepreneur, six-foot tall with a full head of hair, smart as a whip, divorced once, and living in Dallas. Plus he had to be the kind of guy who would think I was the most gorgeous, funny, brilliant woman he'd ever met. Either this man does not exist or even with my mastery of online dating over the period of nine months, I have not found him.

Although I did find my requirements, they didn't all exist in one man. What ensued was a buffet of dating disasters and successes that proved the old adage: Variety is the spice of life. You might discover you enjoy dating men you never would have considered, like a thirty-seven-year-old bail bondsman from Oklahoma who dances like Michael Jackson or a forty-three-year-old toy company executive obsessed with ping pong, or a thirty-one-year-old British geologist with a stiff upper lip and a very sweet tongue. That's what I found anyway.

May I offer some kind advice? Don't be picky. And don't be so damn whiney about how you never meet anyone. Just listen now. We're going to talk about setting up your search with a wide-angle lens. If you receive too many responses, you can always tighten up the search.

These are the common parameters you'll find on most dating sites:

Age of the guy you're seeking

How many years younger or older will you date? When I first started, I said five years younger or five years older, and my prospects were paltry. Now I look at prospects that are fifteen years younger or ten years older, and I've dated many cool guys I would never have met if I'd kept my previous settings. Also some of this came from discovering that I enjoy dating younger men.

Geographic area

You're usually asked to select a radius of miles from your house. For example, you may select that you will date men within fifty miles of your zip code. Most users don't realize there are screens on dating sites that enable them to filter people by distance. You can choose *See Who Is Near Me* and get a list of men one, two, five, or more miles away. This is convenient for checking out the men who live nearby, but it's also really useful when you're on vacation. For example, you might arrive in Rome, click on *See Who Is Near Me*, find a single guy who meets your qualifications, and say "Hey, I'm vacationing in Rome this week. Where should I go for a good lunch today?" Who knows? He might offer to meet you for lunch.

Relationship

This allows you to search by goal. If you're not looking for casual sex, the search engine will filter out men who are. If you have no intention of ever getting married, filter out men who are "putting serious effort into getting married," and so on.

Income level

As tempting as it may sound, I want to encourage you not to search by income level. Here are three reasons:

1. People lie about their income.
2. Often wealthy people choose not to reveal their income for fear of being targeted for their wealth.
3. You are going to miss out on some great men.

Religion

If religion is a very important factor in your life, and your future mate must be the same religion as you, you should use the filter to select this. There are even certain dating sites that are for specific religions.

Ethnicity

If you prefer to restrict your dating to a certain ethnicity, you can set up that filter. You can also widen your search to include certain ethnicities while excluding others. This is another area I encourage you to be adventurous. Consider opening yourself up to new experiences.

Profession

So you'll only date doctors? Way to limit the possibilities. It's OK to search by profession, but don't limit yourself to one or two. No matter what your mother said, there are a lot of great men out there, and they're not all surgeons.

Politics

If it's important that the people you date share your political views, this search can be very helpful. However, I encourage you to stay open to meeting men whose politics don't agree with yours. Mary Matalin and James Carville pulled it off, and I've met plenty of couples with opposing political views who are very happy.

Body Type

You should be inclusive in your filters on this. So you love super fit body builders. Great. But what about that brilliant, handsome, sweet architect who has slacked off at the gym for a couple of years and has a few extra pounds on him? Should you filter him out before you even meet him? The choice is up to you, but experience has taught me that opening up your search to include many men is the right way to start. You can always change your settings later if you wish.

Interests

This is a great way to find men who enjoy some of the same things you do, but don't filter out men whose interests don't perfectly align with yours. You just might discover a new hobby and a sweet boyfriend who opens your eyes to a whole new world.

Chapter 16

It's Your Call:
Making Your Move

If you've followed my instructions so far, you're likely receiving messages from prospective dates. But if, for some reason, you think you've done everything just the way I told you, and you aren't getting enough messages, or messages from the wrong guys, then it's time to take control and make your move. Sometimes you've got to be the huntress.

Now that you've searched through the profiles and found some guys you'd like to date, send them a message. I'll be honest. I've done this many times myself with mixed results. Out of twenty-eight men, only six were with men that I approached. Over time, I learned how to do better searches and get more guys to respond.

So why just six out of the twenty-eight? I think there are a couple of reasons. The men who approached me had already seen my pictures and read my profile. They were interested enough to message me in the first place, which means they were more likely to ask me out. Less than half the men I approached asked me out. When I suggested we might meet, they rarely took the bait. I tested this with all types of men, and my results were the same. You should expect that if you get comfortable with making the approach, you might have the same difficulties I did. There are exceptions to every rule, but in speaking with many other women about their experiences, I've heard this time and time again.

I don't think this is specific to online dating. Men are natural hunters. They enjoy the chase. They might enjoy the novelty of receiving a message from a woman and even like being asked out by a woman, but when push comes to shove, they usually want to be the ones doing the asking.

If you're like me and want to be proactive, go for it. Some sites have options that let you mark his picture as a favorite, click on *Meet Me*, rate his picture, rate his profile, or add his profile to your list of favorites. This may get him to view your profile, but it's never as effective as sending him a message.

Sending a message is the most direct and effective way to get a man's attention on a dating site. Some sites suggest that you send more than one message to make sure he considers you and to improve your chance of getting a response. I don't agree with this tactic. I say one message, and you're done. If he doesn't respond, move on to the next lucky bloke.

So what do you say in your message? First don't click on any automated message buttons like *Show Interest*. Buttons like this generate an automated message like, "Hey there." Most guys who have received one of these before realize it's an automated message and aren't as likely to follow up. Also don't write a message that sounds copied and pasted. For example, "Hi, I like your eyes. I'm Eve." Lame! If he's smart, he'll know you copied and pasted that bad boy.

I've found that, for the first message, longer is not better. One or two lines do the trick. You're just throwing out the bait, trying to get him to check you out and respond if he's interested. Study his profile. Look at all of his pictures. Mention one thing you like about him in the note. I find questions that refer to something in his profile to be particularly effective. "How many times have you been sky diving?" or "How can you not like sushi?!" or "What kind of improvisational theatre do you do?"

I haven't found telling them you have something in common to be particularly effective. Also don't tell them your name in the first note: that way they have a reason to message you back. Remember the only goal is to get them to check you out and respond.

If he does respond, let him take control and drive from there. You can try pursuing him, but when I've tried, it didn't usually end in a date. If a guy wants to date you, he'll make a move in due time. Leave it up to him.

Chapter 17

Getting Good at Being Bad

When I told a colleague of mine about my book, she told me her story. Ariana (not her real name—she'd kick my ass for telling her secret) is a forty-seven-year-old divorcee with no children. She's an executive making a good income, and she lives a contented life in a small town in Texas. Many of her friends find it shocking that Ariana has no desire to get married again or to even have a boyfriend. Not that she doesn't enjoy the company of men—I mean she really likes the company of men, but she doesn't want them around on a daily basis. In fact, she doesn't like seeing the same man more than once.

Of course, nobody in her small town has any idea. They probably think she's a disinterested old maid. Nothing could be further from the truth. Ariana has needs. Sexual needs. And she's found the perfect way to fulfill them.

She doesn't feel comfortable dating for casual sex in her small town because she feels people would judge her. So three years ago, Ariana came up with a plan. She signed up for a dating site, and in advance of her vacation in California, she began scouting for a few nice guys to show her around. After meeting a couple of them, she settled on one she liked, and they spent much of the rest of her trip in bed, on the floor, in the shower, on the sink . . . . You get the picture.

With trysts like these, her trips became pretty darned exciting. Ariana now vacations four weeks a year and never leaves one vacation day unused. She looks forward to her time off from work more than anyone I've ever seen. Ariana bucked what was expected of her and found an adventurous new life. She got good at being bad.

If you're newly sprung from a long-term relationship, and you skipped over all the wild things most people did in their twenties, you're probably chomping at the bit to be a Serial Dater or a Banger. Take notes. I've written this chapter just for you. And take heart—you can do this.

In this day and age, women don't have to choose one man or one marriage for life, and there are many women who have decided marriage simply isn't for them. Some of these women would like to have intimacy and sex as a regular part of their lives, and online dating is a great way to find men who are looking for the same thing.

There are two ways to go about getting good at being bad. If you're a Banger, you can sign up for sites that are for casual sex only. Don't mistake these sites for relationship starters. These sites have one purpose and that is connecting people for casual sex, sometimes referred to as hooking up. Don't expect dinner and a movie before the sex. And don't expect a repeat performance. Sometimes a couple meets this way and decides this arrangement works so well they continue to meet up, but usually, the relationship remains purely sexual.

One of the downsides of joining casual sex sites is that if someone you know sees you on one of them, he might make judgments about you. Yes, I realize if they see you on this site, they're on the site as well, but there's still a double standard. It's a lot more likely a man will get a pass for focusing on his physical needs. I'm pointing this out to help you make an informed decision, not to discourage you. To see an updated list of dating sites and what they offer visit www.GetItGirlGuide.com. For real talk from real women about sex visit www.Sextiquette.com.

An alternative to using casual sex sites is joining mainstream sites and expressing your interest in that kind of relationship. Just select *Casual Sex* or *Hang Out* in the settings. These are settings that will block you from being found by men who are searching the site for relationships. Keep in mind, though, that in some cases, on certain sites, you may be searchable by fewer men.

A less obvious way to show that you're only interested in sex is to select dating options like *Short-term Dating* and use language in your profile headline and description that lets men know you're ready to rock.

Many men who are primarily looking for sex will come out and say so in their settings or profiles. Other men believe taking a more subtle approach works better. I've spoken with many men who say they list "kissing" or "talking about passionate kissing" in their profiles because they think women know this is subtle code for sex. I guess I was pretty naïve when I first started dating again because this was news to me. I love kissing, and reading so many men's profiles that talked about loving to kiss got me excited. *Wow, this is great*, I thought. *All these guys love kissing too!*

Imagine the letdown when I eventually learned kissing was usually code for banging. *Why not just say banging or sex?* I thought. But as I've spoken with many men about this, they say that scares many women away. Perhaps my tastes skew to liking the direct, but subtlety confuses the heck out of me.

Chapter 18

The Catfish:
Don't Take the Bait

Repeat after me because this statement alone can save you a boatload of heartache: "Until I meet someone in person, I do not know if that person really exists."

Earlier we discussed the different types of online dating personalities. Remember the Chatter? That's someone who only wants a virtual relationship and doesn't want to meet anyone in person. I'm assuming you're not a Chatter, and all my advice is focused on looking for a real relationship with a real person whom you will be with in person.

That brings us to the Catfish. A Catfish is someone who is not truthful on dating sites. He (or she) could be lying about a few aspects of his life or could create a completely different identity to fool you. For example, if you were e-mailing or texting with a Catfish, you might assume from his profile that you're chatting with a middle-aged, male construction worker from Connecticut, but in reality, this Catfish could be a retired grandmother in Florida.

I got catfished once. A very attractive, thirty-four-year-old engineer began chatting with me via e-mail on a dating site. His stats looked great: single, no kids, looking for dating/relationship, great job, and good sense of humor. From his profile, I could see he had a big vocabulary (nothing turns me on like a huge, bulging . . . vocabulary).

At the beginning, our chatting was pretty ordinary. He said something nice about my hair and my curves and wanted to hear about my company. I asked him when he'd moved to Dallas and if that was his cute dog in the profile pictures. His responses and more questions came back like lightning, and after three days of very intense messaging, it seemed this guy could have real potential.

We liked the same television shows and books, and we shared similar political views. He didn't have kids but really liked kids. He said he wanted someone he could take out for sushi and have fun dates with. Heck, I love sushi, and I'm super fun. But that was only the beginning. Our e-mail conversations deepened. They were personal, flirtatious, sexual, emotional, intelligent, spiritual, and they went on and on. I had never connected like this with someone online or off, and I was hooked.

After three days of intense chatting, he asked to meet me. I was thrilled. We set up a date for a couple of days later. I asked if we could switch to text, and he said he would rather not until we met in person and hit it off because some girls he had met before had stalked him. *OK*, I thought. *That sounds reasonable.* I asked for his first and last name, as I always do before I meet someone. He gave me his name, told me where he worked, and gave me his personal e-mail address.

I happened to have a good friend who did business with his company, so I called her and asked about him. She did a quick search. "Eve," she said, "that person doesn't exist."

Surely she had made a mistake, I thought. I started investigating. Luckily he had a very odd name which made it easy to search for him online. I came up empty. When I e-mailed him and told him how puzzled I was that I couldn't find him online, he didn't respond.

I logged onto the dating site the next day. His profile had been deleted from the system. If he just hoped to avoid me, he could have simply blocked me. The fact that he disappeared from the site altogether indicated that my note had really disturbed him (or maybe even her). Catfished!

I didn't like it, but I can't say I was devastated. I'd heard about such things happening on dating sites.

Catfish episodes on MTV suggest every catfisher has a different reason for doing what he or she does, including loneliness, shame, vengeance, and fear. I would love to have known what drove my catfish, but understanding the motivations of one won't stop it from happening with somebody else.

Catfishing is cruel, and it hurts to be a victim of it. You have to be smart and remember, "Until I meet someone in person, I do not know if that person really exists." I've heard many people say they don't do online dating because they want to avoid getting catfished. This is a cop-out. Assholes are everywhere—online and off. But there are more good people out there than bad. We have to make calculated decisions and protect ourselves against physical and emotional pain. Finding love requires taking smart chances and being vulnerable yet aware.

These are the warning signs that someone may be a Chatter or worse, a Catfish:

- They seem way too good to be true, and they like all the same things you do.
- They refuse to exchange phone numbers or e-mail addresses with you.
- They avoid meeting you, offer repeated excuses, or stand you up.
- They refuse to send you candid pictures.

- There's lots of chaos in their lives that keeps them from meeting you in person.
- They repeatedly claim to be experiencing bad Internet service, missed calls, or missed text messages.
- They refuse to video chat with you.
- They won't tell you their full name, where they work, or the city they live in, even after a long period of communication.
- Sudden moves out of the area or even the country keep them from meeting you in person.

Let's say you've met someone really great online. You've been chatting with him for a while, and you're sure he's the real deal because you've checked him out. You've also video chatted, seen candid pictures, and talked to him on the phone. However, something stands in the way of meeting in person. Maybe you live too far apart, and neither of you can afford the trip. Sometimes these relationships work out. However, I want you to be careful with your time and your heart.

One woman who thought she'd met her soulmate online has an instructive story to tell. Everything was amazing from the start, she told me. They had the same goals for a relationship, religion, job in the same industry, and same political beliefs and wanted to travel to the same places. Bit by bit, over a ten-month period of communicating online, they fell in love. They had done all the right things—investigated each other, talked on the phone every day, and video chatted often. Finances, children to care for, and work commitments kept them apart. Finally they were able to arrange a visit. He picked her up at the airport, and within twenty minutes, they knew it was a mistake. Virtual love and face-to-face love are two different attractions.

If you have limited time or money, focus your search close to where you live so you can easily meet your prospects. If you have unlimited time and money, fine. Widen your search and meet up early on in the relationship to explore how the two of you feel in person. No matter how great the chemistry is online, you can't use that as a predictor of success. It's ideal to meet a potential mate in person within the first month, especially if you're speaking every day.

Don't invest your heart in a virtual relationship. You'll very likely end up getting hurt. "Until I meet someone in person, I do not know if that person really exists." It bears repeating—often.

Chapter 19

Online Dating:
The Good, the Bad, and the Ugly

I'm drinking a tall latte at my favorite coffee shop, going through my messages on a particular dating site, hitting *delete*, *delete*, *delete*. I could develop carpal tunnel in my index finger with this repetitive motion. Prepare yourself. Do your digital exercises because much of your time on dating sites will be spent deleting messages that are dumb, sick, weird, or simply from undesirable dudes.

I was poised to send the next message to the trash when—hello, Jonah!—I got a message that set off the green light in my brain. "I read your profile, and I'm also a terrible drummer. What kind of company do you have? How old is your daughter? I thought you were stunning, and we live in the same neighborhood. Can I take you out for a margarita?" I didn't waste a second going to his profile: six-feet tall; muscular; forty-one-years-old; boyish-good looks; wavy, brown hair; blue eyes; divorced with one son; good job; fun hobbies; and a great sense of humor evident in his profile summary.

Jonah had done everything right in his message. He showed that he'd read my profile, asked me questions, complimented me, and went in for the close. I appreciate a man who gets straight to the point. Of course, I said yes, and we chatted a bit online before exchanging numbers and moving to the texting phase.

His texting skills were excellent. Good conversation, questions, jokes, feedback, flirting. Soon we settled on a date and met for a beer. Jonah looked just like his pics—heck, maybe even cuter in person. There was some pretty major chemistry between us, and the conversation, though slightly awkward at first, warmed up nicely.

After a long hug and a few quick pecks on the lips in the parking lot, Jonah asked me out on a second date. "Absolutely," I said. Over the next couple of days, the sweet texting continued until one day, in the middle of a rather innocuous text conversation, things went south. Here's how it went:

Eve: "Daddy Jack's is definitely my favorite restaurant in Coppell, but I dig Zenzero for lunch."

Jonah: "I haven't been to Zenzero yet, but I'll have to try it."

Eve: "It is a bakery, but their salads and sandwiches are yum."

Jonah: "I'm lying on the sofa with my giant cock out, stroking it, and thinking about you."

Jonah: "No, wait, no. That message was a mistake. Crap."

Jonah: "Are you there? I'm calling you now."

Jonah called me and went into an elaborate explanation that made absolutely no sense. Jonah was lying, and he was a really bad liar at that. Obviously he was multitexting—texting multiple people at once. This is a fun activity for those of us dating more than one person at a time, but as Jonah displayed, it can be dangerous. Ah, the pitfalls of the digital age.

I didn't go on that second date with Jonah, not because he was sexting with another girl while he was texting with me, but because he lied. That's a deal breaker for me. Maybe I should have given Jonah another chance. He was obviously talented at texting with one hand!

The Online Dating Progression

Now that you're dating twenty-first-century style, your little black book will be your smartphone, and your first contact with a prospective date will be via online chatting. The progression is typically like this:

1. He messages you online.
2. You respond, and the messaging or chatting on the site begins. This period can last a couple of minutes, days, or weeks before the next step.
3. He asks for your phone number so you can switch to texting.
4. The conversation continues via his preferred method—either texting, IM, e-mail, or telephone chats.
5. He asks you to meet in person.
6. You meet up.

If you want to speed up this process, give him your number and tell him you would prefer to text with him. Some men will ask for your instant messaging ID. Occasionally they may ask for an e-mail address.

As soon as you start texting, he will almost surely ask you to send him a picture. Don't send him the same images you have on the site. It can be a head shot or full body, and you should look great, casual, and happy.

Keep three of these photos in your phone to send to new guys. This way, if he asks for a picture, and you're having a super bad hair day, you don't have to worry about it. Sometimes, but not always, he's hoping you'll send him a dirty picture, and depending on your goals and your personality, you may or may not oblige. It's acceptable for you to ask him for a picture too. To make it clear you aren't asking for a dirty one (unless you are), say something like, "Hey, send me a shot of your face for my phone book."

The majority of men prefer to text, but some will actually call you. I've spoken with a lot of women my age and older who aren't big fans of texting and prefer to talk on the phone. I would have thought that older men wouldn't like texting and younger men wouldn't like talking on the phone, but I haven't seen that pattern. I really don't like talking on the phone with someone I haven't met, and I avoid it as much as possible. It just seems like a waste of time. I'd rather text with the guy before I meet him. If we hit it off in person, I'm happy to talk to him on the phone. Not all women are like me. Some prefer getting to know a guy on the phone before they meet him. If that's your preference, speak up and ask.

Video Chat, FaceTime, and Skype

No, FaceTime is not where you get together and sit on his face, you dirty girl! On FaceTime, you use live video to communicate. Skype, Google Hangout, and plenty of others allow you to do the same thing. Men don't request this as often as I would have thought, but the ones that do are pretty adamant about it. I've only done video chat twice with someone I haven't met in person, and I wasn't a big fan of it. The problem is you can't tell if there's any chemistry through a computer screen. If you agree to a video chat, and the guy starts getting naked or asks you to, it's an uncomfortable situation to get out of. But who am I to stop you? You might be up for this.

I do think that video chatting is an excellent option for prospective couples who are separated by a long distance. Let's say you've met someone far away that you can't meet for a while, and you begin to develop a bond. I think video chat is the closest thing to getting together in the flesh, although it's not the same by a long shot. Before you invest in an expensive trip to go meet him, a few video chats would be a great idea.

Another good use for video chat is to catch catfish. If you're talking online with someone in your vicinity who says he's unavailable to meet for a long time, you should be concerned. If you think he's worth the trouble, make sure he's the real deal by asking for a video chat.

You may be tempted and get swept away and get naked or otherwise naughty with someone on video chat before you've even met him. I'm going to encourage you not to do that for several reasons.

Video chats can be recorded.

You could have a fun time on a video chat and then meet in person and have no chemistry. Talk about awkward! Even though your goal may be to meet or date in person, his goal may be just to get some virtual action. Once he's got it, he'll likely disappear or keep coming back for more virtual-only sex. Either way, you lose.

The First Date

So you've met someone interesting online, and you're ready to meet in person. Way to go! We've come a long way together, from overcoming fear and just saying, "Yes!" to creating a kick-ass profile and zeroing in on the Mr. Possibles. Now here you are, getting ready to step out. But wait! Don't be in such a hurry. There are a few things to consider.

First, where do you want to meet? Don't choose a place where you have to order at the counter because then the who-pays decision comes right off the bat, and that's uncomfortable. Plus counter places are often delis, and delis usually have giant pickles, and you might really like pickles as I do. In fact, I'm at the airport right now, eating a big, juicy pickle, and there's an old creeper staring at me. I don't think there really is any way to eat a big, juicy pickle without a dude thinking about you and his pickle. In fact, it's a good decision to stay away from any phallic foods for the first thirty minutes after you meet. No wrapping your mouth around that big dill, no tickling an ice cream cone with the tip of your tongue, and no bananas thrust halfway down your throat.

On a first meeting, never, ever agree to meet at your house—or his. Even if it sounds lovely to have a gentleman offer to come and pick you up, just like in the olden days, resist the temptation to pretend this is an old-fashioned kind of a date. It's not.

That should clear up any questions you might have had about where to meet.

Who pays for the first date? I, for one, never do. I've paid for a third or sixth date because if I've been dating a guy for a bit, I want to take him out sometimes too. I think being the girl gives you the benefit of not paying on a first date and the drawback of having to menstruate. During the fifty-nine dates I went on in my first nine months, when the question came up (this happened three times), I did make the offer, but not one guy took me up on it. I almost always let the guy ask me out, and it makes sense to me that whoever does the asking also does the paying.

Let's say you make it past the first date jitters, you don't eat any of the forbidden phallic foods, and you have a great time. Naturally you can't wait to see him again. Here's where I teach you how to avoid becoming a Stage Five Clinger. If you don't know what that is, put this book down and go watch *Wedding Crashers* right now. Then come back and finish this damn book.

After the first date, let the guy follow up with you. I get that we're in the twenty-first century, and we're living in an equal rights society, but if the guy doesn't call you, he's probably busy or just not thinking about you. Deal with it!

- Do not text him six times in the middle of the night.
- Do not send a friend request on Facebook.
- Do not call him and ask when you are going out again.
- Do not close down your dating profile and ask him when he is doing the same.
- Do not imagine your first name with his last name and write it down in a Lisa Frank notebook.

I know this list seems ridiculous, but people get a little crazy sometimes. After a first date, chill out, and if you like him, hope he calls, and if you don't, hope he doesn't. This can be tough for a modern woman who likes to be in control, but it is what it is, and if you take a more relaxed attitude, you'll be dating guys who really want to see you again. Now doesn't that sound like a good plan?

Chapter 20

Click:
Dating and Your Smartphone

In a national survey, one-third of all respondents indicated they "would be more willing to give up sex for a week than their mobile phone." And 70 percent of those respondents were women! My question to them is, "What kind of sex are you having?" OK, not really. But I would ask, "Where are your priorities?" I would hope that sex is way more fun than playing another game of *Candy Crush* on your smartphone. For the full report on sex vs. smartphones, go to http://www.telenav.com/about/pr-summer-travel/report-20110803.html.

I realize that these days, our phones are a big part of our daily lives. We need to examine the etiquette of cell phone usage during a date. I like to call it sextiquette™— the Emily Post rules of sex in the age of the smartphone.

Thanks to technology, the etiquette of dating and sex has become more challenging. First, when you go out on a date, the place for your smartphone, iPad, Kindle, or other device is in your car or purse. If you have an urgent situation, explain that to your date. "I would not typically keep my phone out because I'm focused on spending time with you. But would you mind if I keep my phone out in case the babysitter needs me? I'll respond only if there's an emergency." Be sure to ask your babysitter to call, not text, in case of an urgent situation. That way, you'll know it's serious.

Here are a few unacceptable reasons for keeping your smartphone out during a date:

- You're waiting for a call back from your hair stylist who does highlights that make you look ten pounds lighter.
- A big business deal could close any minute.
- There's a guy you're talking to who's slightly cuter than your date, and you're hoping he'll text you.

No, No, No! When you're on a date, *he* needs to be your focus. If you aren't paying attention, how can you know if you want to see him again? Plus, being distracted by your phone says his time is not valuable, and that's downright rude.

If your date is distracted by his phone during your first meeting, I wouldn't suggest a second date, unless you really, really like the guy. But you'll have to be bold on the second date and bring up his cell phone addiction, saying something like, "I struggle with putting my phone down too, but I sure would like your undivided attention so we could get to know each other better." If he responds with a rude comment or ignores your request, you can expect him to do the same in other areas of life.

That smartphone is even more intrusive when it comes to sexy time. Here are a few handy rules to remember:

- When clothes come off, turn off the phone.
- If you're getting turned on, turn off the phone.
- When you want to get off, turn off the phone.

Got it? Good.

Sexting

I met Joseph, a forty-one-year-old entrepreneur with his own successful company online. He seemed sweet and super normal. I liked him a lot, even more than I should have since I hadn't met him in person yet. Joseph had a little boy just a couple of years younger than my daughter and that was very appealing to me. I saw the pictures, and he was pretty cute—OK, not stunningly hot but good-looking in a boy-next-door-already-going-bald kind of way.

Joseph and I really enjoyed discussing business, and we had a lot to talk about. We texted endlessly and had lengthy phone calls, but our work schedules kept us from meeting for a week. I was nervous about meeting him, considering how much I liked him. I thought he could have some serious repeat dating potential. Before we met, Joseph started sending a few sexually suggestive texts. OMG! This was something I hadn't experienced.

I called a couple of my girlfriends. "He said he wants to do (beep) with his (beep) to my (beep). Maybe I shouldn't meet this person."

Every one of my single friends reassured me this was normal. "Congratulations," one of them said. "You've received your first sext!"

Wow! I was one naïve thirty-nine-year-old. Sexts! Imagine that!

Before I was divorced, I assumed sexting was strictly a teen activity. I was wrong. Guys from twenty-four to fifty-two have texted me dirty words, pictures, and even videos. I would guesstimate about 30 to 50 percent of men like to sext.

Before you start online dating, you need to decide if you want to participate in sexting. Be ready for an entire variety of dirtiness. Sexting might include mild statements like, "I can't wait to be with you tonight." More advanced sexting would be, "I will lick you like I have never had ice cream before." Super dirty texts say stuff like, "I will taste every bit of your dripping, beautiful pussy."

The first time someone sends you a dirty message, don't freak out. Read it and come up with a reply. If you haven't done it, you just might find you like it. If you don't feel comfortable with this kind of language, tell him you would rather just talk dirty in person. But if you think you might be up for it, tell him you liked it.

Sexting isn't a one-way street. Eventually, it's going to be your turn. You'll have to come up with some dirty talk too. If you're new at this, no worries. I'm here to help. Go to www.Sextiquette.com which will help create dirty stuff for you to say.

Chapter 21

Surprise!
Dick Pics

Yep, I said it. I don't care if you're as pure as the driven snow, if you're online dating, eventually a dick pic is going to pop up on your smartphone screen. You don't want to see that, you say? Men don't care. And, no, I'm not talking about teenagers. Before I was divorced, I would have sworn that texting dirty pictures was something only teenagers and politicians took part in. I was wrong. I have visual confirmation that men in their twenties, thirties, forties, and fifties do it, and, nope, I didn't ask for any of those beauties. You're thinking only a certain class or type of man is doing this. Nope. I've heard about dick pics coming from lawyers, warehouse workers, and every guy on the social spectrum in between.

If you're past thirty and haven't been single for a long time, you'll find this hard to believe. I'm simply trying to prepare you for what your single friends already know. Go ahead and ask them. I'll wait.

I'm telling it to you straight. Men will send you pictures of their dicks. This is another area where perspective is everything. Unless there's a ruler next to that thing, don't believe the hype. Remember, it's likely that objects in the picture are smaller than they appear.

These pictures are going to arrive at inopportune times—during dinner with an important client, for instance, or while your mom is flipping through pictures of your kids on your phone. Right now, before it's too late, get with a tech savvy friend who can set your phone to *preview texts* (thank you, Maria). This setting alerts you to an incoming text and the sender's name. You have to press a button to display the contents of the text. Do this now, not later. You're welcome.

The proliferation of dick pics was a damn shock to me. I couldn't believe it. To this day, I have yet to request such a generous gift, but dick pics continue to arrive on my phone. Sometimes I get a heads up like when a guy texts, "Here comes a pic" or "Here comes a present." Warning: this present is not going to be an actual present. What? Did you expect real flowers to pop out of your cell phone? Nope. I still haven't found an app for that. Other dick pics arrive like rain on a cloudless, sunny day—when you least expect them. They slam right into your face. No warning—just wham!

Dick pics actually inspired my latest entrepreneurial brainstorm. I can't believe I'm going to share my genius business idea with you, but we're girlfriends now, so heck, here goes. Remember Glamour Shots? I think it's time we bring the concept back, but this time it's Glamour Dick Shots. According to my market research, at least 30 percent of all men are an excellent prospect for this product. They all want to make sure their dicks look great in a picture. With Glamour Dick Shots, they'll have an image they can use over and over again. Can you see it? Locations in malls across America, cameras with major zoom ability, and a photographer saying, "It looks good, but it's missing something. Hmmm. I know! A tiny boa! Yes, that's it! Nothing classes up a dick like a boa."

I digress. Sorry. Back to dick pics and you. I know what you're thinking. How do I respond to a dick pic? I searched Emily Post and Miss Manners on this one, and I couldn't find the answer, so let's work through this together, shall we? Here are some sample responses depending on your intentions toward the sender.

If you intend to date him,

- "Wow!"
- "Wasn't expecting that."
- "Did you accidentally send me a pic of your stick shift?"
- "Dick, the other white meat."
- "Cock-a-doodle-doo-me."
- "Is that Ron Jeremy?"
- "How tall do I need to be to ride that thing?"
- "Thanks, but I'd rather see you naked in person."

If you don't intend to date him,

- "Ewwwwwww."
- "I can see something in that pic, but it's too small for me to make out."
- "Did you just go swimming?"
- "Why did you send me a picture of your grandpa's junk?"
- "Thanks. I totally tweeted that pic #Don'tWant-NoShortDickMan."
- "Is it cold there?"
- "I'm gonna pass."

There's one other option that's loud and clear— silence. He'll get the message.

Chapter 22

Your Turn:
Pussy Pics

Sooner or later, some guy is going to ask you for a picture. And that guy won't be asking for your fourth-grade school pic. I'm not saying every guy is fishing for a sexy picture, but it happens way more than you might think.

Before you begin online dating, you have to know your sexy pic level of comfort. It's like deciding how far you'll go with a guy before a date. Don't pretend you don't know what I'm talking about. The first date was great. You kissed the guy, and you're hoping to date him for a while. Before you go out with him again, you decide how far you'll let him get. If you're like me, you'll set up self-protective boundaries like not shaving your legs or wearing your ugly green underwear with the holes so you won't let him take your skirt off, even when things get really fun and you're super tempted. Setting up your rules for what you will do in sexy pictures is the same thing. Set your boundaries and stick to them.

Before you decide on your comfort level, remember, this is the digital age. Any picture or video you give to someone could be seen by thousands of others—accidentally or on purpose. In a flash, you could be famous or worse, infamous. Heck, just look at Kim Kardashian—her entire tawdry career began with a sex tape. Actually don't look at Kim Kardashian. Her example may not make my case because she turned that little so-called mistake into a moneymaker that I doubt any of us could match with our dirty digital assets.

Think of it this way: Any dirty picture you share digitally could end up being seen online by your mom. Does that clear it up? Should you share dirty pictures? Maybe so. Your Mom has probably seen a few sexy images in her time, and somehow she did create you, didn't she?

Here are the levels of dirty picdom. Which one sounds the most like you?

G-rated

You like to project a Pollyana image. You rarely, if ever, wear clothes that show cleavage. You're in a profession that involves children or religion or politics or some other sensitive area that would preclude revelation of your body parts. If anyone saw you naked besides your lover, you would absolutely die of shame and regret. Your life would be over. If this sounds like you, just say, "No." If he insists and you really like the guy and want to send him some kind of treat, consider sending him a picture in something body hugging—workout clothes, a tight dress, or even a bathing suit. If he persists and asks to see body parts, simply say, "Nope, I don't do that." If he moves on, good riddance.

PG-13

You're a bit saucy, but you're a smart, careful girl. You'd rather naked pictures of you didn't end up being tweeted or posted on Facebook. You may be a professional, but in you're profession, you wouldn't be judged harshly if you cursed at the office or wore a sleeveless shirt. Although you will rarely send a stranger a dirty picture, you aren't averse to a little play with the man in your life. You won't get naked in a picture, but you will put on that sexy orange and pink bra and panty set, get your body at just the right angle, and send your man a shot of what's in store for him later that night. Also if you're out with the girls one night, looking particularly hot in a short skirt, you make sure to get someone to take a nice picture from the back so he can see the badonkadonk he's missing. You figure your mom has seen you in your underwear a time or two, so if she should happen upon your sexy pictures, what the heck. Plus you really like your body, and your face isn't in the shots to give you away.

R-rated

You're comfortable going topless on nudist beaches and consider the human body a thing of beauty. There's no shame in showing it off. Hell, yes, you send interested men tastefully done, naked pictures. In many of your shots, you're completely naked, but they're more sug-gestive than revealing. You wouldn't be ashamed if these pictures ended up online because they're more artistic than pornish. To entice your target, you use props, good lighting, and outfits that show off your whole body, and you never include your face in the pic.

NC-17

Your mom doesn't need to know a damn thing about what you do with your body. You think your pussy is a blue-rib-bon-prize winner, and it needs to be shown off as much as possible. But you're an exhibitionist with a brain, and you never include your face or other identifying features in the picture like your full name surrounded by roses tattooed on your ass. Your entire body is never in one image, just parts, like a box of fried chicken—a breast, a thigh, and the real money shots like the bare ass or the full-on pussy unfiltered in all its glory. Some NC-17ers—not the smart ones—include their faces in the pictures because they just know their man would never share. Beware!

X-rated

You don't talk to your mom, or if you do, she curses like a sailor, cigarette dangling from her lips and tells you dirty jokes. You couldn't care less if she saw you naked online. You're already a porn star or a stripper, so what the hell? You post pictures of your full body, all parts, including your face, and you fully expect these pics are going to end up online or in the hands of someone you've never met. But dammit, shouldn't you get paid for those beauties? To each her own.

Decide where you fall now, so you can let your dating prospects know what to expect upfront (pun intended). When they ask, give them what you've got and don't be talked into violating your boundaries.

Never include your face in naked, sexy pictures. Want a little more deniability should your pictures make it onto the World Wide Web? Invest in a two-dollar brown or black eyeliner pencil from the store. When you get ready to take a naked picture, color on a fake mole and presto—plausible deniability. "What? Those aren't my huge, fantastic tits! This woman has a mole next to her right nipple, and I most certainly do not!"

Here's one of my favorite lines for men who continue to pester me for dirty pictures. "I don't do dirty pics. I get dirty only in person, and only if I like you a whole heck of a lot."

Beyond that, I have a tool for those rare but rude men who repeatedly ask for a picture of your pussy. If they can't take no for an answer, and you'd like to have a little fun, the next time a guy asks you to text a picture of your pussy, give him what he wants. Use your phone camera and take a shot of pictures like these and text him descriptions like the ones you see beneath each picture here. You'll also find fun pics you can use for free to text to your man at www.GetItGirlGuide.com or www.Sextiquette.com.

Now these are pussy pics everyone can enjoy!

Wet Pussy

Hairy Pussy

Feisty Pussy

This Pussy isn't going to lick itself.

Sweet, Young Pussy

Hairless Pussy

More Pussy Than You Can Handle

Chapter 23

Safe Sex:
The Ins and Outs

Congratulations! You have a wonderful man who is ready to play. And you're a grown woman who respects herself and values her health. It's condom time!

I was shocked to discover that many men our age don't have condoms with them, and if they do, they refuse to put them on. As the world struggles to educate young people on the dangers of unsafe sex, it seems that the adults haven't learned the lesson yet. I'm going to assume you've heard of sexually transmitted diseases, and you're committed to protecting yourself from them. Celibacy is the only way to ensure total protection, but I believe many women would like to be sexually active, and that means wrapping his junk up like a present without the bow.

You shouldn't have to convince a man to put on a condom, but if that's what it comes down to, simply assure him that he's not getting in until the condom goes on. Don't be ashamed to have condoms in your purse, on your bedside table, or wherever else you need to have them to be prepared. Buy a variety of types if you want, and sure, stock up on those extra-large condoms, although, let's be realistic, a lot of those are never going to get used. Here's what I hear happens when average-sized guys put on condoms designed for the well-endowed. The condom slips off mid-bang and ba-boom, you've just been exposed to the great unknown. Buy the extra-large ones if you must and stash them in the back of the drawer where they will sit until that special occasion when you unwrap a super big, unexpected present.

Don't rely on condoms alone for birth control. They're not 100 percent effective. (Yep, I learned that fact on *Friends* like you.) See your doctor about the right form of birth control for you. Never take a man's word that he's had a vasectomy. I've heard stories of men saying this simply to avoid wearing a condom. Yep, the world is a crazy place.

If this is your first foray into condom use, practice putting them on bananas or cucumbers so you'll be prepared to help out. Just don't buy really big cucumbers—I don't want you to feel let down when the real item presents itself.

When you find someone amazing, and the two of you are ready to enter into a committed relationship, it's time to go—together—to get tested for STDs before engaging in unprotected sex. Visit your own doctors or consult our list of resources for discounted testing at www. GetItGirlGuide.com or www.Sextiquette.com.

It's not much fun to think about STDs and unwanted pregnancies, but it's absolutely necessary to practice safe sex. Protecting yourself will provide you with years of many happy returns and happy endings!

Chapter 24

Dating in the Real World

Now that you've ventured out beyond the virtual into the world of real, live men, there are a few areas I'd like to cover. I just can't bear the thought of sending you out there unarmed and a danger to yourself.

Speed Dating

This may or may not be for you. I first heard of speed dating when I was married, and since I'm impatient as hell and like things that go fast—fast cars, fast flights, fast business deals—it totally made sense to me that I would enjoy speed dating.

As soon as I was divorced, I signed up for a speed-dating event which allots about five minutes with each guy before he moves on. This is a brilliant idea because, if the guy is lame, five minutes is over in a flash. On the other hand, if the guy is great, it's enough time for the two of you to figure out you'd like to chat more. At the end of the night, you write down who you want to give your number to, and if the guy picks you too, you take it from there.

In preparation for my first speed-dating event, my friend Maria helped me shop for a new outfit—leather skirt, red heels, and a black and silver shirt that showed off two of my best assets nicely. Here's what I was going for: "I'm sexy and available, but I'm not a ho."

I was looking pretty damn cute, but there was one problem. I was not in the correct mindset for speed dating. It was Valentine's Day, and I had just stopped seeing a guy I really liked. In retrospect, I realize how desperate this sounds, but at the time, I was just looking for a fun experience.

Let me tell you something. Speed dating is not fun. Funny, but not fun.

When I arrived at the bar, a singles mixer was also going on. I decided I should check out the male merchandise there first. If men were handbags and I was shopping for a nice Fossil clutch, I found only cheap, fake-leather knockoffs that night.

Not finding something relaxed, classy, slightly high-end, but reasonable at the singles mixer, I headed over to the speed-dating event and scanned the men on that side of the room. Hmm, what do we have here? Short, bald guy; tall, Indian guy; skinny, black guy; a smattering of look-alike white guys; a snappy dresser in a wheelchair; a total nerd; and two exceptionally-well-dressed guys who were awfully touchy feely with each other.

Next I checked out my competition. What kind of woman would speed-date on Valentine's Day? Oh, wait. Crap. Someone like me. I began comparing myself to the others, which any therapist will tell you is the fast lane to crazy town. I was one of the larger women there, but there was one, thank goodness, who was much bigger. Though I was one of the cuter girls there, I didn't appreciate the two women who looked like rock stars. One of them, a tall, young Diana Ross type, should have been required to operate with some kind of handicap as they do in golf. Maybe she shouldn't have been allowed to wear deodorant, or her feet should have been a size twelve double D, anything to give the rest of us a chance. Of course, there was the obligatory, sexy Asian girl in a dress so small I swear my daughter had one just like it for one of her Barbies—in the same size. Aside from them, though, I felt as if I fit right in with the twenty other women in attendance.

The speed-dating leader explained the rules. We would talk for five minutes and then move on to the next date.

All right! I'm ready to rock!

The first guy was so boring I wouldn't remember if he was a green alien. The cute, tall Indian guy came next. I prepared to charm him, but I couldn't get a word in edge-wise. In the first three minutes, he told me how serious he was about his strict religion and how much he would like to see me strip. Naturally I was confused and didn't say much when it was my turn to talk. He did request my number later. Perhaps I'm quite attractive to certain men when I shut up.

Next was the short, white guy. He had patches of gray hair and patches on the elbows of his sweater, so I'll call him Patches. This guy brought his A game. He liked me, and he let me know it right away.

> **Patches:** "I think you should go out with me because I have a really good job."
>
> **Me:** "Well, that's nice. What do you do?"
>
> **Patches:** "I'm the produce manager at a grocery store, and it's nonstop excitement." (There was no sarcasm here; I know sarcasm when I hear it.)
>
> **Me:** "What is exciting about your job?" (I'm thinking, *why is he talking about this job like he's the pilot of Apollo 18?*)
>
> **Patches:** (He's burning with enthusiasm and can't get the words out fast enough.) "Just

about everything. Do you know how amazing heirloom tomatoes are? There are so many varieties. And rhubarb—you really have to take extra care of rhubarb. Lettuce has to be placed a certain way so it doesn't get crushed. And melons, oh, melons. Don't even get me started on melons!"

Unfortunately, our time was up before he could get started on melons. Whenever I'm at the grocery store, I think fondly of Patches and what could have been.

One contender told me he didn't really want to spend five minutes talking to me because I had my own company, and he was just a software engineer. Another guy couldn't shut up about the latest installment of the *Star Wars* trilogy.

One half of that friendly guy couple I had mentioned earlier sat down next to me. "Girl, you are working that hair!" he exclaimed. Did I just see him snap back and forth? I swear I did. He soon went off with his buddy, who'd been chatting up another unsuspecting victim. I'm still confused by that whole situation.

After the gay guy, there were some real jerks, but once you start the speed dating process, you have to go through all the members; otherwise, you'll leave some poor schmuck sitting there alone for five minutes wondering what's wrong with him.

So, as I continued, if someone was rude, I had a little fun. I highly recommend trying this should you go speed dating and someone is rude to you:

> **Speed Date Dude:** "Hey, I'm Tommy."
>
> **Me:** "Hi, Tommy. I'm Eve."
>
> **Speed Date Dude:** "So what are you trying to get out of this?"
>
> **Me:** "Uhm, to meet someone nice I might like to date."
>
> **Speed Date Dude:** "Yeah, whatever." (He looks as if he is distracted, uninterested, and suffering through a root canal, so I decide to shift gears and have some fun.)
>
> **Me:** "Know what I really like?"
>
> **Speed Date Dude:** "No."
>
> **Me:** "Cats! I love cats. Especially when they are little and cute but when they are big too but in a different way. I have five cats but I'm. . . ."
>
> **Speed Date Dude:** "You have five cats?"
>
> **Me:** "Yeah, I have five cats, but I'm totally gonna get some more soon 'cause I think seven would be better. Don't you think that sounds much better? Five is kind of a weird number for the

way cats bond, and I think in my tiny apartment seven would make them feel much better. My favorite cat is Gloria Steinem; she really has a lot of attitude. Ohhh, but do you know what I like even more than cats?"

Speed Date Dude: "What?"

Me: "Unicorns!"

Speed Date Dude: "Unicorns?"

Me: "Yes, Unicorns! I mean don't worry. I totally know that unicorns aren't real. Well, probably not real, who can ever really say anything doesn't exist for sure, right? That is what miracles are all about." (Pause for dramatic effect and stare off into space. Throw in a subtle eye twitch if you've got the talent). "But I just love the way unicorns have that pretty white coat that reflects light in a sort of rainbow way, and their horns are so majestic. Whenever I see a picture of a unicorn, I can't resist snapping it up. I don't think people realize how artistic and important unicorns are to the world. Oh, my gosh, I have an amazing idea. I should dress up Gloria Steinem as a unicorn this year for Halloween. Wouldn't that be amazing?"

Shockingly that guy didn't ask for my info. By the way, I can't stand cats, I don't live in an apartment, and I stopped being into unicorns when I was nine years old, but damn, the look on his face was priceless, and I ended up having a great time that night. There was no one I was interested in, but I came home with a great story for my girlfriends, and we died laughing.

Speed dating definitely requires a sense of humor, and that's something you're going to need for a lot of situations you'll run into in this dating game. The point of all this is to meet guys and to have as much fun as possible in the process. That's not going to happen if you stay in your house watching *Mary Tyler Moore* reruns. Go out. Have drinks with friends, go to concerts, take classes, try meetups, speed dating, singles mixers—anything that gets you out of the house. And when you're dating situations don't turn out as planned, don't take this as a personal failure. Take it as a learning opportunity and another chance to have some fun.

Younger Men

Have I talked about my first cougar moment? No? I was probably saving the juiciest for last.

His whimsical picture was adorable, and he picked me up online by agreeing to my posted request for someone to watch *Shark Week* with. Then I saw his age: twenty-four years old. You've got to be kidding me. I'm not good with math, but I'm pretty sure there was a fifteen-year age difference. That's just too much. (Do you think a man would have these thoughts about a younger woman? Heck, no. He'd jump at the chance.)

I told him he was too young for me.

"How old would you like me to say I am?"

Nice comeback, I thought. I began to chat with Henry, and the more we talked, the more I liked him. He also had skills of pursuit that I find sorely lacking in many men these days.

Henry wasted very little time before asking me out, and when I said I wasn't sure, he reassured me. "If age is the only thing holding you back, what's the harm in meeting me?"

He walked into the swanky bar where we'd agreed to meet, and I thought he was a real cutie, though not my usual type. I'm attracted to a chiseled jaw. His was rounded. I like men with short hair. His was wavy and past his ears. I like a guy with confidence bordering on cockiness, and boy, (pun intended) did he have a boatload of confidence!

Henry had a big vocabulary—always a turn on for me—and he had a quirky sense of humor. Best of all, he knew how to pay attention to me. He tried to hold my hand right off the bat. I pulled it away and told him I thought he was sweet but that just wasn't going to happen. Apparently Henry's high school debate classes were still fresh in his mind because he put forth a barrage of good arguments for pursuing a relationship. I was confused. I usually know right away if I want to continue, but he was so young and so different, I just couldn't figure it out.

After a lot of waffling, I finally made this offer: "You get one kiss. If the chemistry is good, we'll have another date. If not, we'll just be friends."

"No problem," he said, confident—cocksure—as ever.

And then he kissed me, and my mind took off: *Twenty-four! He's only twenty-four! What would his mom think? Oh, God. How old is his mom? Am I ready to be a cougar?*

I pulled away. "I'm sorry," I said. "We're just going to have to keep it friendly."

I thought he was being very sweet and accepting as he walked me back to my car. He said goodbye, and then, before I knew what was happening, he grabbed my hair roughly, pulled me close, and kissed the hell out of me.

Talk about taking control! He kissed every uptight thought right out of my head. When he looked into my eyes and whispered, "How about we do this my way now." I was completely under his spell. He kissed me harder and pressed his body against mine—the way only a fully grown man can do.

There was another date the very next night. And the next . . . .

The Last Word on Sex, Love, and Online Dating

Now that you know everything about my nine-month online dating experiment, from the down and dirty to the high flyin', it's your turn. No worries. We've come this far together, and I'm not going to leave you. We're girlfriends now, and we stick together.

Though I've stopped counting my dates, you can bet your new Victoria's Secret push-up bra I'm going to continue dating and enjoy every minute. Just like a couple of chicks curled up on the couch, sipping a glass of wine, catching each other up on the latest crazy, thought-he-was-a-ten dude, we're going to stay in touch. I'll be sharing my experiences with you at www.GetItGirlGuide.com, and that's where you'll be telling us your own online dating stories. Trust me. If you've followed my detailed instructions, you'll have plenty.

www.GetItGirlGuide.com will also be a great place to check out dating sites. It features a rating system that will help you find the ones that work best for you. Be sure to give your feedback too. What goes around comes around. Help a sister out.

Here's another thing I want you to think about. If you haven't already, it's high time to take charge of your sexual desires and fulfillment. You deserve a safe place to ask questions on the subject. That's the purpose of www.Sextiquette.com. You will get answers to the naughty questions you're too embarrassed to ask your friends. You'll also find a glossary of sexual terms that you can turn to when your new boyfriend wants to "snowball" or "daisy chain" and you have no idea what he's talking about. Plus when you've decided to be playful and do a little sexting, www.Sextiquette.com will help you with some hot and funny ideas on what to say.

If it weren't for the journey I've decided to take myself on I would have missed laughing hysterically with my girlfriends over way too much champagne and so many dirty stories. I would have missed taking off a man's shirt and realizing I could have braided his back hair. I would have missed text messages that included words and pictures so dirty they shocked me. I would have missed having barbecue that was quite delicious while a man spoke about his ex in-laws for two hours straight. I would have missed incredibly fun dates that I would never have expected because these weren't the type of men I'd typically go out with. I would have missed watching Golden Girls with my date and turning it into a drinking game where we had a drink every time Blanche talked about sex or Rose talked about St. Olaf. I would have missed the date with a new guy while my date from the week before glared at me across the room. I would have missed going on a date to the drive-in movies and feeling as if I were 16 every time my date held my hand and kissed me. And I would have missed that night when we talked for six hours straight, and danced in my kitchen to old hip hop music; then he took me in his arms.

I know you're nervous about all this, but I promise, if you decide to take this journey with confidence and a sense of humor, you're in for one heck of a good time and possibly more. It's your life. Don't miss it.

Top Ten Tips for Online Dating Success

1. Online dating can be a bitch. Make it your bitch!

2. Stop putting everyone else first. Put yourself first, and go for it.

3. Run toward fear with your Fearless Alter Ego.

4. Set Your Relationship Goal, and act with that goal in mind.

5. Expand your horizons. Try some flavors of men you've never considered before.

6. Tell the truth in your profiles about who you are and what you want, and keep your pictures within six pounds and six months.

7. Develop and use your USP—your Unique Selling Proposition.

8. Play it safe with private information, dating locations, and sex.

9. Remember that until you meet someone in person, you do not know if he really exists.

10. Expect good things to happen, and when unexpected, gross things happen, take the opportunity to tell your friends and laugh your ass off!

Appendix 1

The Stats

Sources: Reuters, *Herald News*, *PC World*, *Washington Post* (Data verified 6/18/13)

http://www.statisticbrain.com/online-dating-statistics/

Online Dating Statistics	Data
Total number of single people in the US	54 million
Total number of people in the US who have tried online dating	40 million
Total eHarmony members	20 million
Total Match.com members	15 million
Number of questions to fill out on an eHarmony survey	400
Annual revenue from the online dating industry	$1.049 billion
Average spent by dating site customer per year	$239
Average length of courtship for marriages that met online	18.5 months

Online Dating Statistics	Data
Average length of courtship for marriages that met offline	42 months
Percent of users who leave within the first 3 months	10%
Percent of male online dating users	52.4%
Percent of female online dating users	47.6%
Percent who say common interests are the most important factor	64%
Percent who say physical characteristics are the most important factor	49%
Percent of marriages in the last year in which the couple met on a dating site	17%
Percent of current committed relationships that began online	20%
Percent of people who believe in love at first sight	71%
Percent of women who have sex on the first online dating encounter	33%
Percent of people who say they have dated more than one person simultaneously	53%
Percent of sex offenders who use online dating to meet people	10%

Online Dating Facts
A woman's desirability online peaks at 21
At 26, women have more online pursuers than men
By 48, men have twice as many online pursuers as women
Men lie most about age, height, income
Women lie most about weight, physical build, age

What's More Important on a First Date	
Personality	30%
Smile and looks	23%
Sense of humor	14%
Career and education	10%

Type of Hair Color Most People Are Attracted To	
Blonde	32%
Brown	16%
Black	16%
Don't Mind	16%
Red	8%
Bald	8%
Gray	4%

Girls Prefer	
Nice guys	38%
Bad guys	15%
Blend of both	34%
Any man I can get	6%

Guys Prefer	
The modern career girl	42%
The girl-next-door type	34%
The hottie	2%

Pew Research Center (Internet & American Life Project-Dating, 10/21/13) (Data collected 2005-2013) http://pewinternet.org/topics/Dating.aspx?typeFilter=5

2005 Data vs. 2013 Data

- In 2005, only 43% of daters actually went on a date with someone they met online.
- In 2013, 66% of daters went on a date with someone they met online.
- In 2005, 15% found long-lasting relationships.
- In 2013, 23% now find long-lasting relationships.

2013 Stats

- 1 in 10 Americans has used an online dating site or mobile dating app.
- 11% of American adults have used online dating sites, including 38% of American adults who identify as "single and looking for a partner."

- 66% have gone on a date with someone they met on a website or app.
- 23% have met a spouse or long-term partner through these sites.
- 5% of Americans who are currently married or in a long-term relationship met their partner somewhere online. Among those who have been together for 10 years or less, 11% met online.
- 54% feel that someone else seriously misrepresents themselves on their profile.
- 28% have been contacted via a dating site in a way that made them feel harassed.
- 59% see online dating as a good way to meet people.
- 53% say it is a good way to find a better match.
- 42% of American adults say they know someone who has used online dating.
- 29% of American adults say they know someone who has married or entered a long-term relationship through the sites.

Appendix 2

Dating Sites

Here is a list of 50 online dating sites with information gathered at the time of publication along with why you might like each site. An updated and more comprehensive list is available at www.GetItGirlGuide.com.

Website	Description	Free to Interact	Cost	Browse for Free but Does Cost	Tagline
match.com	There are millions of members on this site. There are daters here who are searching for long-lasting relationships. You can narrow down your matches by age, location, body type, religion, eye color, and more. Virtually unlimited options for finding the perfect mate.	No	$39.99 per month.		You like things big! No, not that, you dirty girl. I mean dating sites. Match.com is one of the biggest.
eHarmony.com	eHarmony boasts more marriages than any other matchmaking service. Offers expert guidance on matching, with extensive questionnaire to help you find your match. Your profile is created personally for you, and it offers insights into who you are and how others perceive you—as well as what your needs are in a partner. You can search for compatibility or get matched through the compatibility test.	No	$59.99 per month. But you can usually get a deal.		Wedding bells are ringing in your ears. Because of compatibility testing this site says they have more people getting hitched than other matchmaking services.

Website	Description	Free to Interact	Cost	Browse for Free but Does Cost	Tagline
howaboutwe.com	User base of over 1.5 million singles looking to go on fun dates. Post a date, get connected, and go! Puts focus on the date rather than the individual. Users propose fun activities. Other users can send them messages if they like their ideas.	No	To send such a message costs $7.99 and $34.99 per month depending on how long you commit.		Even though you are doing online dating, you don't like it, and those stallers who don't want to meet in person make you nuts.
zoosk.com	Rapidly-growing platform. Caters to all ages, but is attracting younger audience because of the tie-in to social media. Connect through your Facebook account. There's no sign-in hassle.	Yes			You like Facebook a whole bunch and want a dating site that ties in with that. You also find cheesy pick-up lines hilarious.
chemistry.com	Very large user base drawn from match.com, with members seeking a serious relationship and long-term commitment. You take the free personality test and get matched with dozens of compatible partners within your area.	No	Not free, but join and you get three months free.		You enjoyed taking the Myers-Briggs test at work and would like a site that finds matches based on your personality testing.
fastcupid.com	Fast, easy way to meet singles. Sign on with Facebook account for quick access and view other Facebook Fastcupid accounts.	Yes			You are a Facebook lover, and you don't have a lot of patience.

perfectmatch.com	If you're seeking your perfect match, this is the site. Featuring millions of registered members, Perfect Match is packed with hundreds of features which make it stand out from all the other dating sites.	Yes			You want a dating site with a bunch of nifty features.
matchmaker.com	Great for mature individuals ages thirty-five and over and looking for serious long-term relationships, not just casual dating.	Yes			You played Q*bert or Pole Position as a kid, so you are thirty-five or older, and you're ready to settle down.
lavalife.com	Choose from thousands of local members in your area. Different communities to explore.	No	Seven day free trial. $34.99 per month. $18.99 per month for three month membership.		You don't want to have to drive far to meet your date.
spark.com	Focuses on providing the highest quality online dating experience from day one by requiring that all members take a short but detailed personality test called the Color Code. Requires all members to have a photo and allows all members to respond to e-mails.	No	Less than $40 per month, but free to browse.	Yes	Your aura is lavender, or you like tests that involve colors. You won't go out with someone unless they have a picture posted.
friendfinder.com	Registration procedure is clear and simple, and once you have joined, there are lots of interesting profiles to browse through—all with pictures. Quickly find many people you are interested in getting to know. Won't cost you anything.	Yes			You like things free and easy. No, I'm not talking about your date! :)

Website	Description	Free to Interact	Cost	Browse for Free but Does Cost	Tagline
getiton.com	Find a partner with whom you can hook up and share intimate fantasies. Gives you the opportunity to chat and meet with sexy individuals who have the same sexual preferences you do. Whether you are looking for a single-night sexual encounter or a lasting relationship, you will find thousands of steamy options.				The name says it all. You want to get it on, and I don't mean your pants.
alt.com	For the super kinky singles seeking bondage, fetish, and BDSM. This site has tons of singles looking to get into some hard, rough, and naughty sexual desires.	Yes			*Fifty Shades of Grey* is your favorite book, and you need to be tied up tonight!
christianmingle.com	An online community created specifically for Christian singles looking to find friends, romance, or marriage.			Yes	Jesus is your homie, and your mate should feel the same.
adultfriendfinder.com	If you are looking for something more intimate than just a date, check it out. You will find thousands of like-minded adults with sexy photos, seeking affairs, discreet relationships, and sexual encounters. There are also individuals who are looking to date in general.			Yes	You are a Banger, so let's get to bangin'!
date.com	Date.com has a scientific matching system that calculates perfect matches by comparing your profile with over 10 million active members. To determine your best match, they use your information, based on over fifty profile attributes, and use their matching algorithm—fancy!	Yes		Yes	You like a little scientific matching to your dating site.

silversingles.com	For singles fifty and over, in their prime, ready to meet for friendship, dating, and marriage. Provides online dating services, including online personals and photographs.		Yes	You already got that AARP membership even though you certainly don't feel that old!
passion.com	If you're tired of going on the same boring dates, this site will really liven things up.		Yes	You are a passionate person ready to put that passion to the test.
matemakers.com	A safe, friendly community of singles. Also provides dating tips and a free newsletter. They also say that they don't have any old profiles that have been around for ages, only the most recent ads.	Free for women.		You are sick of old, outdated profiles crowding up a site.
sparkology.com	To join the site, you must be a college graduate. Men must be verified graduates of a school on the site's list of "top universities." Men have to invest each time they communicate and are less likely to do so when they aren't sincerely interested.	Women pay a flat fee per month to be on the site. Men pay a small fee to start conversations, which theoretically prevents them from spamming everyone on the site.		You want an educated man and only want to have conversations that are likely to truly go somewhere.

Website	Description	Free to Interact	Cost	Browse for Free but Does Cost	Tagline
social.nerve.com	Users post mini updates on their profiles that answer simple questions such as "What did you do last night?" Whether they read a book, saw a concert, or watched TV, the hope is that it will give others a reason to connect.	No	Unlimited messaging costs $20 per month.	Yes	You like telling about and hearing about daily details.
singlesaroundme.com	SinglesAroundMe is an Android, BlackBerry, and iPhone app. It uses the GPS feature on your phone to find singles near you, literally plotting them on a map.	No	$2.95 per month or $19.95 per year.		You love your smartphone and want to find singles so close to you that you could ride a bike over to their place.
soul2match.com	Soul2Match promises to match singles based solely on one piece of information from each of them: their headshot. No long questionnaires. Simply upload a photo and match your soul mate.	Yes			You like judging a book by its cover.
joingrouper.com	Grouper arranges group dates for three women and three men. Uses Facebook and other details to maintain their interesting member community.	Yes			First dates on your own make you nervous. Group dates are your thing.
mate1.com	One of the busier online dating sites, Mate1.com reports that they have over 29.5 million users and tens of thousands more joining each day.		Women are able to use the site for free, while men must pay a fee to use the message center and chat.		You dig free sites but want men to pay to play.

outtime.com	OurTime.com is an online dating site aimed at mature singles. Unlike many other dating sites, it's refreshingly clean and well-structured. If you are over fifty and looking for a long-term relationship, marriage, companionship, or simply a pen pal, OurTime will help you find that special someone.		Membership is free, but members must upgrade to a paid account to use all of the site's features.		You remember Woodstock, and you want a serious mate or a pen pal.
cupid.com	Cupid.com is a dating site that takes a more natural approach to finding love. They encourage their members to search for potential partners who match their inner spiritual needs and desires and let love come naturally.		Forum and basic messaging and search services are free. Members must upgrade to access advanced features.		You believe love comes from within, and you don't like to rush things.
bbpeoplemeet.com	BBPeopleMeet is a plus sized singles site.	Yes	One month for $14.95 per month, 6 months for $9.95 per month.	Yes	You've got a little extra meat on your bones and want to date guys that do too.
pof.com	A chemistry test matches you with personalities that lead to long-lasting, stable relationships. Matches are made to meet your emotional needs.	No	$9.95 per month.		You enjoy personality tests and want lots of guys to choose from.

Website	Description	Free to Interact	Cost	Browse for Free but Does Cost	Tagline
lovestruck.com	Designed to help you find other singles who live or work near you. You can find out who likes what you like via their date ideas tool.	No	Free, but must upgrade for interacting.	Yes	Location, location, location! Your prospective dates have to be close by.
mysinglefriend.com	No profile writing because they believe that your friends know you best. They write your profile for you. Just like having a virtual wingman by your side, it takes the hassle and stigma out of dating and paints a better picture of you as a person. Your friends can even recommend other singles on the site to you, and it doesn't matter who starts the process. Your friend can add you, or you can join up and simply give them your friend's e-mail address.	Yes	Upgrade to access all features.		You simply cannot write that darn profile, and so your friends write it for you!
true.com	With over 30 million singles, True.com is one of the largest dating sites on the web today. True.com was created by dating experts who wanted to bring a powerful, fully featured dating site to the public that also rejects married people and screens for sex offenders.	No	$49.00 per month.		You want your prospect to be pre-certified like a preapproved credit card. Members here are run through a check system for making sure they are not married.

personaldatinga-gent.com	Their secret is to make things so simple that all you'll have to do is show up at the date. They take care of every step, from creating your profiles to organizing your dates. This way, you enjoy the pleasures of real-life dating, without any of the Internet hassle.	No	$300 for the basic package.	You've got money, and you want someone to do all this online dating work for you.
mingle2.com	Find dates, lovers, or friendship totally free on AOL's dating service.	Yes		I didn't actually realize AOL was still around, but apparently it has a dating site that is free.
speeddate.com	SpeedDate is about creating real-time interactions with five minute speed dates. They connect you with local singles who are online and ready to chat. You control who you talk to and when.		Check site for monthly membership rates.	You feel five minutes of interaction will tell you if someone is dateable or not.
tastebuds.fm	The founders of Tastebuds noticed they always met the most awesome new people through music–in bars, at gigs, or just talking to people about the bands they love.	Yes		You love Salt-N-Pepa, and he loves the Doobie Brothers?! This site matches you by your taste in music.
beautifulpeople.com	Connects you with beautiful men and women in your local area and from around the world. You meet real, beautiful people who actually look in real life as they do online.	Yes		You believe looks are damn important. If he is a ten in the pic, you want him to be a ten in real life.

Website	Description	Free to Interact	Cost	Browse for Free but Does Cost	Tagline
datehookup.com	For everyone, including seniors, whites, blacks, Asians, Latinos, and everyone else.	Yes			You are up for lots of quick chats with potential for "hooking up" or dating.
benaughty.com	Meet up and flirt with thousands of singles in your area. Enter flirty chat rooms and chat online people who are eager to find other singles for exciting all-night adventures. Meet new people, flirt without serious intent, enjoy webcam sessions, and mingle with other singles in the realm of naughty fantasies.		Check the site for monthly membership rates.	Yes	You are a naughty girl who wants a playmate online, on webcam, or in person.
singleparentmeet. com	Single moms and dads can find interested and interesting parents searching for romance. Designed to help single moms and dads navigate the difficult world of dating for parents.		Membership required.		Mommy wants to date!
datingforparents. com	A dating service for single men and women with kids who are ready to start over and find someone right for them.		Joining is free, but full access requires an upgrade.	Yes	Time to create the Brady Bunch!
carrotdating.com	A site for people who believe gifts are the greatest ice breaker. Carrot Dating turns "fat chance" into "why not?" From flowers to jewelry, there's a bribe for everyone's budget.		Membership required.		You believe bribery is good, and in this case, even fun!

checkhimout.com	Checkhimout.com puts the power in women's hands. The environment of the site leaves it up to women to make the first move.	Yes	Free for women, but to interact, men must pay.	You are tired of being approached by lots of undesirable guys, and you want the power!
herway.com	At HerWay, women's profiles are invisible by default. This innovative approach to dating allows women to browse for men anonymously instead of being bombarded by unwanted attention, ensuring 100% privacy.		Membership required.	Girl Power! Here you pick who you want to talk to not vice-versa.
cosmopolitandating.co.za	This dating site is for fearless women. You find your perfect match with the help of the leading ladies magazine, *Cosmopolitan*.	Yes	Free	Cosmo has saucy stories, so why not a free dating site to get things going?
millionairemate.com	Meet talented and successful men who've achieved wealth and status and are eager to share the benefits of a fabulous lifestyle with you. Date with confidence—their wealth verification system helps you find the right man.		Membership required for full access.	Yes	You are a gold digger. OK, maybe not, but you still want a rich dude.
sugardaddie.com	Connects you with someone to have fun with for one night or for a long-term relationship.	No	$20 per month.	You are looking for a successful guy to have fun with tonight or for longer.

About the Author

Eve Mayer is a divorced mom and humorist who is an experienced online-dating enthusiast. After fourteen years with one man, Eve ran toward her fear to embark on a whole new digital world of dating. She dove in head first going on 59 dates with 28 men in 9 months, walking away with experiences that shocked her, thrilled her, and just plain cracked her up. Eve speaks professionally on the topics of online dating and women empowerment and has spoken for Tedx on "The Fearless Alter Ego."

Before focusing on the subject of dating, Eve started out as CEO of www.SocialMediaDelivered.com where she was recognized by *Forbes* as one of the 20 Most Influential People in Social Media. Eve writes, speaks, and consults worldwide on the subject of using social media to achieve business goals and is the author of "The Social Media Business Equation." She is known as @LinkedinQueen on Twitter. CNN named Eve "One of the Eight Women to Follow on Twitter in 2013."

Eve lives in Dallas, Texas, with her seven-year-old daughter Mia and is probably going out on a date tonight.